Under
the Midnight
Stars

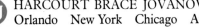 HARCOURT BRACE JOVANOVICH, PUBLISHERS
Orlando   New York   Chicago   Atlanta   Dallas

Under the Midnight Stars

ODYSSEY An HBJ Literature Program

Sam Leaton Sebesta

Consultants

Elaine M. Aoki	Carolyn Horovitz
Willard E. Bill	Myra Cohn Livingston
Sonya Blackman	Daphne P. Muse
Sylvia Engdahl	Barre Toelken

ISBN 0–15–333354–5

Acknowledgments

For permission to reprint copyrighted material, grateful acknowledgment is made to the following sources:

Addison-Wesley Publishing Company, Inc.: ''I Am Rose'' from *The World Is Round,* © 1939, renewed 1967, by Gertrude Stein, A Young Scott Book.

Atheneum Publishers: ''Mean Song'' from *There Is No Rhyme for Silver* by Eve Merriam. Copyright © 1962 by Eve Merriam. ''''Let's Marry!' Said the Cherry'' with accompanying illustrations from *Let's Marry Said the Cherry and Other Nonsense Poems* by N. M. Bodecker. (A Margaret K. McElderry Book). Copyright © 1974 by N. M. Bodecker. Illustration accompanying ''The Fly in the Rye'' from *Let's Marry Said the Cherry and Other Nonsense Poems* by N. M. Bodecker. (A Margaret K. McElderry Book). Copyright © 1974 by N. M. Bodecker. By permission of Atheneum Publishers.

Blackie and Son Limited: ''Twelve Months'' from *Russian Fairy Tales* by Moura Budberg et al.

William Collins Publishers, Inc. and *Jane Yolen:* Adapted from *The Emperor and the Kite* by Jane Yolen. Copyright © 1967 by Jane Yolen. Illustrations by Ed Young from *The Emperor and the Kite* written by Jane Yolen. Reproduced with the permission of William Collins Publishers, Inc. Copyright © 1967 by Ed Young.

Thomas Y. Crowell: ''Gently, gently, the wind blows'' from *I See the Winds* by Kazue Mizumura. Copyright © 1966 by Kazue Mizumura.

Doubleday & Company, Inc.: Adapted from *Amelia's Flying Machine* by Barbara Shook Hazen. Copyright © 1977 by Barbara Shook Hazen. ''I Go Forth to Move About the Earth'' by Alonzo Lopez from *The Whispering Wind* edited by Terry Allen. Copyright © 1972 by the Institute of American Indian Arts.

E. P. Dutton: ''Winter Walk'' from *Street Poems* by Robert Froman. Copyright © 1971 by Robert Froman.

Norma Farber: ''Spendthrift'' by Norma Farber from *Cricket* magazine, © 1976 by Norma Farber.

Grosset & Dunlap, Inc.: ''A very fat snowman'' from *The Big Book of Limericks* by Edward Mullins. Copyright © 1968 by Edward Mullins.

Harcourt Brace Jovanovich, Inc.: ''The Big Wind of '34'' abridged and slightly adapted from *Grandpa's Farm,* © 1965 by James Flora. Excerpted from *Rufus M,* copyright 1943, 1971 by Eleanor Estes. ''Theme in Yellow'' from *Chicago Poems* by Carl Sandburg, copyright 1916 by Holt, Rinehart and Winston, Inc.; copyright 1944 by Carl Sandburg. ''Winter Night'' from *The Golden Hive,* copyright © 1962, 1966 by Harry Behn.

Harper & Row, Publishers, Inc.: Adapted text and illustrations from *Stevie* by John Steptoe. Copyright © 1969 by John L. Steptoe. Adaptation from *Old Arthur* by Liesel Moak Skorpen. Text copyright © 1972 by Liesel Moak Skorpen. ''Spring'' from *In the Middle of the Trees* by Karla Kuskin. Copyright © 1958 by Karla Kuskin. ''The Fourth'' from *Where the Sidewalk Ends* by Shel Silverstein. Copyright © 1974 by Shel Silverstein.

Holt, Rinehart and Winston, Publishers: ''Talk'' from *The Cow-Tail Switch and Other West African Stories* by Harold Courlander and George Herzog. Copyright 1947, © 1975 by Holt, Rinehart and Winston.

Houghton Mifflin Company and *George Allen & Unwin Ltd.:* ''Oliphaunt'' from *The Adventures of Tom Bombadil* by J. R. R. Tolkien. Copyright © 1962 by George Allen & Unwin Ltd.

Alfred A. Knopf, Inc.: From *The Cat Came Back* by Dahlov Ipcar. Copyright © 1971 by Dahlov Ipcar. ''In Time of Silver Rain'' from *Selected Poems* by Langston Hughes. Copyright 1938 and renewed 1966 by Langston Hughes.

Little, Brown, and Co.: From ''Adventures of Isabel'' from *Many Long Years Ago* by Ogden Nash. Copyright 1936 by Ogden Nash. ''The Grasshopper'' from *Far and Few* by David McCord. Copyright 1952 by David McCord. *Just the Thing for Geraldine* by Ellen Conford. Copyright © 1974 by Ellen Conford.

Macmillan Publishing Co., Inc.: ''March'' from *Summer Green* by Elizabeth Coatsworth. Copyright 1948 by Macmillan Publishing Co., Inc., renewed 1976 by Elizabeth Coatsworth Beston. ''Maurice's Bear'' (retitled) from *Maurice's Room* by Paula Fox. Copyright © 1966 by Paula Fox.

Macmillan Publishing Co., Inc., The Trustees of the Tagore Estate, and *Macmillan, London and Basingstoke:* ''Paper Boats'' from *The Crescent Moon* by Rabindranath Tagore. Copyright 1913 by Macmillan Publishing Co., Inc., renewed 1941 by Rabindranath Tagore.

Parents' Magazine Press: Adaptation of *Mrs. Beggs and the Wizard* by Mercer Mayer. Text copyright © 1973 by Mercer Mayer. Illustration copyright © 1973 by Mercer Mayer.

Philomel Books: Illustration by Ed Young from *The Emperor and the Kite* by Jane Yolen, reprinted with the permission of Philomel Books. Illustration © 1967 by The World Publishing Co. Illustration by Ed Young from *The Emperor and the Kite* by Jane Yolen, reprinted with the permission of Philomel Books. Illustration © 1967 by The World Publishing Co.

Playboy Magazine: ''Not Me'' by Shel Silverstein. Originally appeared in *Playboy* magazine. Copyright © 1960 by Shel Silverstein.

G. P. Putnam's Sons: "The Beach" from *The Adventures of Mole & Troll* by Tony Johnston, illustrated by Wallace Tripp. Text copyright © 1972 by Tony Johnston, illustrations copyright © 1972 by Wallace Tripp.

Random House, Inc.: From *My Father's Dragon* (retitled *My Father and the Dragon*) by Ruth Stiles Gannett. Copyright 1948 by Random House, Inc.

Marian Reiner: "Discovery" from *Whispers and Other Poems* by Myra Cohn Livingston. Copyright © 1958 by Myra Cohn Livingston.

Paul R. Reynolds, Inc. 12 East 41st Street, New York, N.Y. 10017: "Eat-It-All Elaine" from *Don't Ever Cross a Crocodile* by Kaye Starbird. Copyright © 1963 by Kaye Starbird.

Scholastic Book Services, a Division of Scholastic Magazines, Inc.: From *Rumpelstiltskin* retold by Edith H. Tarcov, illustrated by Edward Gorey. Text copyright © 1973 by Edith H. Tarcov. Illustrations copyright © 1973 by Edward Gorey.

Scott, Foresman and Company: "Fall" by Sally Andresen from *Reflections on a Gift of Watermelon Pickle . . . and Other Modern Verse* by Stephen Dunning, Edward Lueders and Hugh Smith. Copyright © 1966 by Scott, Foresman and Company.

United Feature Syndicate, Inc.: "Snoopy" (retitled) from *You'll Flip, Charlie Brown* by Charles M. Schulz. © 1966 United Feature Syndicate, Inc.

Viking Penguin Inc.: From *Along Sandy Trails*, text by Ann Nolan Clark and photographs by Alfred A. Cohn. Text copyright © 1969 by Ann Nolan Clark. Photographs copyright © 1969 by Alfred A. Cohn. All rights reserved.

Frederick Warne & Company, Inc.: From *Dance of the Animals*, copyright © Pura Belpré 1972.

Art Acknowledgments

Willi K. Baum: 211 left; Chuck Bowden: 120, 163, 191, 209 (adapted from photographs from the following sources: 120, courtesy UPI; 163, courtesy Harcourt Brace Jovanovich, Inc.; 191, courtesy Pura Belpré); Diane de Groat: 99; Bert Dodson: 120–121, 122; Sharon Harker: 40, 41, 42, 100, 101 top, 102–103 top, 210–211 top, 212 top; Ed Taber: 32, 145, 210 bottom, 211 right, 212 bottom, 317; Don Weller: 232.

Cover: Richard Brown.

Unit openers: Jane Teiko Oka.

Contents

1 It's Not Funny

Just the Thing for Geraldine

A story by Ellen Conford
Pictures by Ed Taber

There was nothing Geraldine liked better than hanging by her tail from the branch of a tree and juggling a few acorns.

But her parents told her there was more to life than juggling, so every week she went to Mademoiselle La Fay's School of the Dance to learn ballet.

"It will help you to be graceful," said her mother.

"It will help you to be ladylike," said her father.

"It will help you keep physically fit," said her brother Randolph.

"Nothing could help her," whispered her brother Eugene.

One day Geraldine came home from ballet school very excited.

"Everybody come look!" she shouted. "Come look at what I can do!"

"What is it?" asked her mother.

"We learned the Dance of the Purple Swan," Geraldine said.

"That's wonderful!" said her mother.

"A whole dance!" exclaimed her father. "And you haven't even been going to dancing school very long."

"Swans aren't purple," said Eugene.

"Now, watch me," Geraldine ordered. "Are you looking?"

"We're looking," said her mother.

Geraldine smoothed down her tutu, which her mother had made for her out of leaves, and gracefully raised her forepaws over her head.

"Dee, da da da da dee ta dum," she hummed, and ran lightly, on tiptoe, around the trunk of the tree.

"Oh, how beautiful," sighed her mother.

"Encore, encore!" clapped her father.

"That's pretty good, Geraldine," said Randolph.

"Can we go play now?" asked Eugene.

"Dee, da da da da ta dum," Geraldine hummed, and began to dance faster around the tree.

But one of the big roots of the tree was sticking up from the ground and Geraldine didn't see it.

"Ow!" yelled Geraldine, as she tripped over the root and sprawled on the ground.

"Did you hurt yourself?" asked her mother worriedly.

"No," Geraldine sniffled, and ran up the tree before Randolph and Eugene could see her tears. She hung upside down by her tail, her leafy ballet skirt covering her face.

"I see you, Randolph," she said angrily. "You think I can't see you, but I can. You'd better stop laughing."

Randolph covered his mouth with his paw.

"I'm not laughing," he said, trying to sound serious.

"Is it all right if *I* laugh?" asked Eugene.

"There is nothing to laugh at," their father said sternly.

"Geraldine just tripped," their mother said. "It could happen to anyone."

"Especially Geraldine," whispered Eugene to Randolph.

"I heard you, Eugene!" Geraldine shouted. "You think I can't hear you, but I can!" She pulled herself back up on the branch and straightened her tutu. "I'd like to see *you* do the Dance of the Purple Swan."

"Swans aren't purple," said Eugene. "Swans are white."

Randolph and Eugene went back to their game. Geraldine took off her ballet skirt. She looked at it thoughtfully as she folded it and put it away.

The following week, when Geraldine came home from ballet school, her mother and father were waiting for her.

"Well, what did you learn at dancing school today?" her mother asked eagerly.

"I learned," Geraldine said unhappily, "that I am not a very good dancer."

"Nonsense!" said her father. "You dance beautifully. And you haven't even been going to dancing school very long."

"And I don't think I'll be going much longer," said Geraldine.

"Oh, of course you will," said her mother. "You'll see, you'll be a graceful dancer in no time."

Geraldine shook her head.

"No, I won't," she said. "I cannot do *pliés* and *arabesques,* and when we're supposed to dance on our toes my toes curl up and I fall down. I am just not cut out for ballet."

"But I thought you liked ballet school," said her mother.

"I like juggling better," said Geraldine.

"But don't you want to learn to be graceful?" asked her father.

"No," said Geraldine, swinging back and forth by her tail from the branch of the tree and juggling some pebbles. "Not really."

"Oh," said her mother.

So, her mother signed her up for a class at Schuyler's School of Sculpture.

"I'm sure you have artistic talent," said her mother.

"Sculpture school is just the thing for you, Geraldine," agreed her father.

"I don't know," said Geraldine, doubtfully, as she flipped three blackberries in the air and balanced a twig on the end of her nose.

"Oh, you'll see," said her mother. "You'll make bowls and pitchers and artistic statues. Sculpture school will be lots of fun."

Every week Geraldine went to Schuyler's School of Sculpture, and every week her parents asked, "How do you like sculpture school?"

And every week Geraldine shrugged and said, "It's okay, I guess."

One day Geraldine came home from class carrying a big pile of something wrapped in wet leaves.

"What's that?" asked Randolph.

"That's clay," said Geraldine.

"What's it for?" asked Eugene curiously.

"We have to make a sculpture of someone," Geraldine said.

"Oh, boy!" cried Eugene, jumping up and standing very straight and flexing his muscles. "Do me, Geraldine, do me!"

"We just have to do the head," Geraldine said.

"Oh," said Eugene, disappointed. "Well," he brightened a minute later, "do *my* head." He turned his head sideways so Geraldine could see his profile. "I have a nice head. Please, Geraldine?"

"You have to sit very still," Geraldine warned. "You can't move around or wiggle or anything."

"I won't," promised Eugene. "I won't even blink."

Geraldine sat Eugene down in front of her and turned his head sideways. She unwrapped the mound of clay and put it on a tree stump. Randolph sat down next to her.

"Don't sit there and watch me!" Geraldine snapped. "How do you expect me to concentrate when you're staring at me like that?"

"You're very touchy," said Randolph. "Why are you in such a bad mood?"

"I'm not in a bad mood!" yelled Geraldine. "Now, go away and leave me alone!"

Randolph went off to play ball and Geraldine began to work on her sculpture.

After a while, Eugene began to squirm.

"Is it finished yet, Geraldine?" he asked.

"No," said Geraldine.

"My nose itches," complained Eugene.

"Sit still and be quiet!" Geraldine ordered.

Geraldine molded the clay, squeezing it, poking it, and muttering to herself while she worked.

"What are you saying, Geraldine?"
Eugene asked. "I can't hear you."

"I'm saying 'stupid clay!'" Geraldine
snapped. "Now will you be still? How can
I sculpt you if you keep wriggling around?"

"I can't help it," Eugene whined. "I'm
getting tired. My neck hurts. And I think I
have to sneeze."

"Be quiet. And I'm doing your mouth
now, so please keep it shut."

Eugene sighed. Geraldine went on
molding and muttering.

Finally she said, "There. It's done. I
think."

"Oh, good!" said Eugene, jumping up and stretching. "I feel stiff all over. Let's see it."

But Geraldine was covering her sculpture with the wet leaves.

"Let me see it," Eugene said. "Why are you covering it up? I want to see my head."

He ran over to the tree stump and began pulling off the leaves.

"Stop it!" yelled Geraldine, swatting at him. "You stop that, Eugene! I don't want you to look at it. I don't want *anybody* to look at it."

"I won't hurt it," Eugene said, yanking off the leaves. "I want to see it."

Randolph and their mother and father came running when they heard Eugene and Geraldine.

"What's going on?" asked their father.

"Why are you two screaming like this?" asked their mother.

"*What* is *that?*" Randolph asked, pointing toward the tree stump.

Eugene had pulled all the leaves off Geraldine's sculpture and was backing away from the tree stump, shaking his head in fury.

"That is *not* me!" he howled. "I don't look like that!"

"Well, if you didn't move around so much—" Geraldine shouted.

"Is *that* supposed to be *Eugene?*" Randolph asked.

"It's . . . it's very interesting," their father said weakly.

"It is not interesting!" shrieked Eugene. "It's a bunch of lumps! I don't look like a bunch of lumps!"

Geraldine sighed, and began to cover up her sculpture with leaves again. When she finished covering it all up, she climbed the tree and hung by her tail, swinging gently back and forth as she juggled some pine cones.

A little while later Randolph and Eugene came up the tree and sat down next to Geraldine.

"You sure are a good juggler, Geraldine," said Randolph kindly.

"Thank you," Geraldine murmured.

Randolph gave Eugene a poke in the ribs.

"Ow! I mean, oh," said Eugene, "I wish I could juggle like you can."

"Do you really?" Geraldine asked.

"You're the best juggler we know. ISN'T THAT RIGHT, EUGENE?" said Randolph, glaring at his brother.

"Yes," Eugene said.

"So we'd like you to teach us how to juggle," Randolph said. "WOULDN'T WE, EUGENE?"

"Yes," Eugene said.

"Oh," said Geraldine, happily, "of course I'll teach you. It's not too hard, once you get the hang of it. Now, just watch me and——"

"Geraldine!" her mother called. "I've thought of just the thing for you!"

"What is it?" asked Geraldine.

"Singing lessons!" her mother said excitedly. "How would you like to take singing lessons?"

"No," said Geraldine, juggling her acorns.

"No?" her father asked. "But you'd love singing lessons."

"No," repeated Geraldine. "I wouldn't."

"But, why not, Geraldine?" asked her mother.

"What if I'm not a good singer?" said Geraldine. "I took ballet lessons and found out I wasn't a good dancer."

"And you certainly aren't good at sculpting," Eugene added.

"She sure is a good juggler, though," said Randolph. "And nobody ever gave her juggling lessons."

"That's true," their mother said.

"I never thought of that," said their father.

"Neither did I," said Geraldine.

Suddenly, she stopped juggling and jumped up.

"I'll be right back," she said, and ran down the tree.

In a little while, Geraldine returned. She was lugging a big piece of wood.

"What's that?" asked Randolph.

Geraldine propped the wood up against the trunk of the tree.

"Come and look," she said proudly.

The possums came down from the tree.

"I made a sign," said Geraldine.

"What kind of a sign?" asked Eugene. "What does it say?"

"Oh, it's beautiful," said their mother.

"Aren't you the clever one!" said their father.

"What does it *say?*" cried Eugene. "Tell me what it says!"

"It says," Randolph told him, "GERALDINE'S JUGGLING SCHOOL."

Questions

1. What were two things Geraldine could *not* do well?

2. What was one thing Geraldine *could* do well?

3. What was funny to Eugene but *not* funny to Geraldine?

4. Geraldine had a *talent* for juggling. What is a *talent*?
   a. A wish to learn something.
   b. An ability to do something well.
   c. A pile of acorns and pine cones.

Activity

If you started a school, what would you teach best? Draw or paint a sign for your school. Your sign should tell the name of your school and what you will teach.

"Let's Marry!" Said the Cherry

Poem and pictures by N. M. Bodecker

"Let's marry,"
said the cherry.

"Why me?"
said the pea.

"'Cause you're sweet,"
said the beet.

"Say you will,"
said the dill.

"Think it over,"
said the clover.

"Don't rush,"
said the squash.

"Here's your dress,"
said the cress.

"White and green,"
said the bean.

"And your cape,"
said the grape.

"Trimmed with fur,"
said the burr.

"Won't that tickle?"
said the pickle.

"Who knows?"
said the rose.

"Where's the chapel?"
said the apple.

"In Greenwich,"
said the spinach.

"We'll be there!"
said the pear.

"Wearing what?"
said the nut.

"Pants and coats,"
said the oats.

"Shoes and socks,"
said the phlox.

"Shirt and tie,"
said the rye.

"We'll look jolly,"
said the holly.

"You'll look silly,"
said the lily.

"You're crazy,"
said the daisy.

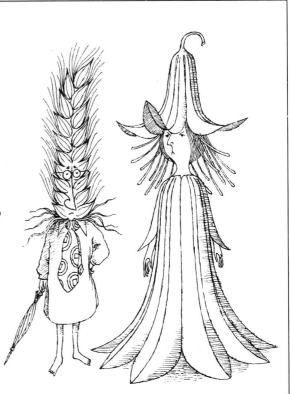

"Come, let's dine,"
said the vine.

"Yeah—let's eat!"
said the wheat.

"And get stout,"
said the sprout.

"Just wait,"
said the date.

"Who will chime?"
said the lime.

"I'll chime!"
said the thyme.

"Who will preach?"
said the peach.

"It's my turn!"
said the fern.

"You would ramble,"
said the bramble.

"Here they come!"
cried the plum.

"Start the tune!"
cried the prune.

"All together!"
cried the heather.

"Here we go!"
said the sloe.

"NOW—let's marry!"
said the cherry.

"Why me?"
said the pea.

"Oh, my gosh!"
said the squash.

"Start all over,"
said the clover.

"NO WAY!"
said the hay.

Learn About

Poetry

Rhyming Couplets by **Myra Cohn Livingston**

When two things or two friends go together, you can call them a couple. In poetry, when two lines that rhyme go together, they are called a *rhyming couplet* (KUHP•lit). The sound that ends the first line is repeated in the second line. Rhyming couplets are fun to hear, and they are easy to remember.

Here are two rhyming couplets from the poem "'Let's Marry!' Said the Cherry" by N. M. Bodecker.

This is a rhyming couplet.

This is a rhyming couplet, too.

"Let's marry,"
said the cherry.

"Why me?"
said the pea.

In the first couplet, the word that ends the first line is *marry.* It rhymes with *cherry,* the last word in the second line. What are the rhyming words in the second couplet?

Poets often use rhyming couplets in their poems. Some are long poems. Some are short. Gertrude Stein uses only two couplets in her poem "I Am Rose."

I am Rose my eyes are blue
I am Rose and who are you?
I am Rose and when I sing
I am Rose like anything.

Blue and *you* are the rhyming words in the first couplet. What are the rhyming words in the second couplet?

Rules for a Rhyming Couplet

1. Two lines must come one after the other.
2. The end words of both lines must rhyme.

Remember these rules!

Read these poems. Which ones have
rhyming couplets? What are the rhyming words?

1. **Discovery**

   Round and round and round I spin
   Making a circle so I can fall in.
                —Myra Cohn Livingston

2. A peanut sat on a railroad track,
   His heart was all a-flutter.
   The five-fifteen came rushing by—
   Toot! toot! peanut butter!
               —An American folk rhyme

3. "What's the news of the day,
   Good neighbor, I pray?"
   "They say the balloon
   Has gone up to the moon!"
                —An old rhyme

Try writing some rhyming couplets
yourself. Begin with two couplets. Then
perhaps you'll try writing a longer poem.

Mean Song

A poem by Eve Merriam

Snickles and podes,
Ribble and grodes:
That's what I wish you.

A nox in the groot,
A root in the stoot
And a gock in the forbeshaw, too.

Keep out of sight
For fear that I might
Glom you a gravely snave.

Don't show your face
Around any place
Or you'll get one flack snack in the bave.

Picture by Susan Jaekel

The Beach

A play adapted from the story by Tony Johnston
Pictures by Wallace Tripp

Characters

Storyteller 1   **Storyteller 2**   **Mole**   **Troll**

Storyteller 1:   Mole and Troll went to the beach.
They felt the warm sand
between their toes.

Storyteller 2:   They felt the warm sun on their backs.
When it got too hot,
they sat by the tide pools
and dangled their toes in the water.

Storyteller 1:   Suddenly, Mole jumped up!

Mole: You pinched me!

Troll: I did not!
I was sitting here dangling my toes
and minding my own business.

Mole: Well, maybe your business is pinching.
There is no one else around.

Storyteller 2: Troll made a face. He did not like
being called a pincher.
No one said anything for a little while.

Storyteller 1: Then Troll felt a pinch on his toe.

Troll: OU-OU-CH! Stop that pinching, Mole.
Just because someone pinches you,
you do not have to pinch me!

Mole: I did not touch you!

Troll: You did! You did! You *did!*
There is no one else around.

Mole: Look, Troll, it is too nice a day
for arguing.
Let's enjoy the sea
and forget this silliness.

Storyteller 2: So they sat and enjoyed the sea.
The salt mist touched them and felt cool.
Sea gulls flew by,
and everything was calm.

Storyteller 1: Then Mole cried out.

Mole: YI-I-IKES!
You did it again, you fuzzy troll!

Storyteller 2: Troll felt a pinch, too.

Troll: It was you!
This time you pinched me so hard,
you made a little red lump. Look!

Storyteller 1: Mole leaned over to look
and there was a little red lump.

Mole: I did not do that. You have a hive.

Troll: How can I have just one hive?
Hives come in bunches!

Mole: I don't know! But you do!

Troll: All right, we will sit very still
with our hands on our heads
and *see* which one is pinching.

Mole: You are sneaky,
because then you will pinch
with your feet.

Troll: Then we will sit very still
with our hands on our heads
and our feet in plain sight.

Mole: Okay, Troll. We will do that.
But I am sitting on seaweed
to protect myself on all sides.

Troll: Then so am I.

Storyteller 2: So they sat very still
on big seaweed piles
with their hands on their heads
and their feet in plain sight
to see who was pinching.
They sat like that for a long time.

Storyteller 1: At last Mole said,

Mole: Troll! It is too still.
Nothing is happening.
There is something funny about this.

Storyteller 2: Someone else thought it was funny, too.
Someone else giggled very loudly.

Storyteller 1: It was a big crab.
He had been doing the pinching.
They looked so silly
that he could not help giggling.
Mole and Troll chased him,
but he ran into a tight hole
and giggled for half an hour.

Troll: Mole, I am sorry for shouting at you.

Mole: Me, too. And I would never pinch you, because you are my friend.

Troll: Me, too.

Storyteller 2: Then they went swimming in a place where there were no crabs at all.

Questions

1. Why were Mole and Troll arguing?

2. What did Mole say that made Troll angry?
   a. "Let's enjoy the sea."
   b. "I did not touch you."
   c. "I am sitting on seaweed."

3. What did Mole and Troll do that showed they were happy with each other again?

4. Mole said that Troll had a *hive.* What is a hive in this play?

Activity

What might have happened if Mole and Troll had not heard the crab giggle? Tell how they could settle their argument. Write what Mole and Troll might have said to each other.

Mole: _____

Troll: _____

Maurice's Bear

From the story *Maurice's Room* by Paula Fox

Pictures by Bert Dodson

Dead beetles, scraps of wood, a plate of worms, salamanders—these are just some of the things that Maurice keeps in his small room. Maurice is proud of his collection. Unfortunately, his parents don't enjoy it as much as he does. Maurice found most of the things on his own, and his friend Jacob gave him the rest. This morning, Maurice and Jacob are going to pick up a large, stuffed bear that Mr. Klenk, the building janitor, has stored in the basement of their apartment building.

One Saturday morning, Maurice awoke at six o'clock. His window was blurred because it was raining so hard. The hamster stirred in its cage.

"You're up too early," Maurice said. The robin lifted one wing slowly and opened its good eye. Maurice went into the kitchen and made himself a sandwich. It felt good to be eating a sandwich and walking down the hall so early in the morning. No one else was awake. He gave a piece of bread crust to the robin and one to the hamster. Then he got dressed.

Soon there was a soft knock on the front door. It was Jacob, who always arrived early on Saturday mornings and who usually brought something with him. Today he was carrying a paper sack.

"Do you want a sandwich?" asked Maurice. Jacob nodded. Then he showed Maurice what he had brought in the bag.

"What is it?" asked Maurice.

"I think it's for weighing things. I found it in a box on the street," Jacob said, holding up a large white scale. The paint was chipped, and when Maurice pressed his hand down on the platform, the needle on the dial jiggled.

"Your arm weighs six pounds," said Jacob.

Maurice's mother walked by. She was
yawning. She glanced into the room. "Good
morning, children," she said.

"My arm is very heavy," said Maurice.

"That's nice," said Maurice's mother, and
yawned again and walked on.

"I forgot to tell you," Jacob said. "Mr. Klenk
said to come and get the bear."

Maurice put the scale on his bed. Then both
boys ran to the front door and down the five
flights of stairs to Mr. Klenk's room in the
basement. Mr. Klenk was blowing on the cup of
coffee he was holding in one hand. He carried a
broom in the other.

"It seems I hardly have time for coffee," said
Mr. Klenk. "I'll be glad to get rid of that bear."

He left them standing at the door, peering
into his room. In a minute he was back, pushing
the bear before him. The bear's feet were
strapped into roller skates. It was as tall as Jacob.

"Here he is," said Mr. Klenk. "Think you
can handle him?"

Jacob and Maurice stared. The bear was
plump. Its fur was black. Its two front paws
stuck out straight in front of it. The claws were
of different lengths, and some of them pointed
upward as though the bear had been pushing
against a wall.

"Why is it wearing skates?" asked Maurice.

"It came that way," said Mr. Klenk.

"It looks tired," said Jacob.

"It had a long sea voyage, all the way from
South America."

Maurice pulled and Jacob pushed and they got the bear up the stairs all the way to Maurice's front door and inside. Because of the skates the bear moved easily on a level surface, but it had been a slippery business getting it up the stairs.

"I think we'd better wait a while before we show it to my mother and father," said Maurice. "They don't like surprises."

"Mine neither," Jacob said.

Maurice said, "Why don't you get your hat and coat and put them on the bear and maybe they'll think it's you if we push him down the hall fast."

Jacob went to get his outdoor clothes. They dressed the bear, pulling Jacob's hat almost all the way down its muzzle. Then, running, they pushed it down the hall. As they went by his parents' bedroom, Maurice's father poked his head around the door.

"Who's that?" asked Mr. Henry in a sleepy voice.

"Jacob!" said Maurice.

"Maurice!" said Jacob.

Mr. Henry went back to bed. "You shouldn't roller-skate in the house," he said.

At last they got the bear into a corner of Maurice's room. "The bear has a funny smell," said Jacob.

"You're right," said Maurice. "But we'll have to get used to it."

They took Jacob's clothes off the bear. Then they stood and looked at it. It was pleasant to have a big animal in the room with them, even if it was stuffed.

"Maurice," Mrs. Henry called. "Come and drink your apple juice."

"We'll have to disguise it. Then one day when they're feeling good I'll just tell them I have a bear," said Maurice in a whisper. Then he called out, "We'll be there in a minute."

"Couldn't we hide it under the bed for a while?" asked Jacob.

"No," said Maurice. "It won't fit because the Victrola's there. But wait a minute." Maurice opened his closet door and pulled out a heap of clothing. Pretty soon he found what he wanted. It was a penguin costume.

"It was for Halloween," said Maurice.

They started dressing the bear. They had to cut holes in the feet to fit the costume over the bear's roller skates. Then they zipped up the front and pushed the bear between the table and the window. Nothing was left showing of it except the big bumps where its paws were. Then they went to the kitchen and had apple juice and doughnuts.

The next day, which was Sunday, Maurice's uncle was coming to visit. When Maurice heard that his uncle's big dog, Patsy, was coming with him, he went to his room and began to pile up things behind his door.

Maurice's father knocked, and Maurice opened the door a crack.

"Maurice," he said, "you'll have to clean out the hamster's cage. There's a very strong smell coming from your room."

"All right," said Maurice. "I'll do it right now." He looked at the bear in its penguin costume. "I wonder if I could spray you with perfume," he said.

Then he took a piece of rope and tied one end of it around the bear's neck and the other to his bedpost. If somebody came in, he decided, he would just roll the bear out the window and then pull it back into the room when the coast was clear.

A few minutes later, he heard his mother let his uncle in at the front door.

"Well, Lily, how are you?"

"Fine, and you?"

"Fine, and your husband?"

"Fine, and Patsy?"

"Fine."

"Fine," said Maurice to the hamster.

"And how is Maurice?" asked the uncle.

"Fine," said his mother.

"He'll be delighted to see Patsy."

"He surely will be delighted."

Maurice added his boots to the heap behind his door.

A large object suddenly hurtled down the hall and against Maurice's door. It was Patsy. The barricade gave way, and Patsy raced into the room, stomping and huffing and panting. The snake slid under its rock, the lizard froze, the hamster burrowed in its sawdust, and the bird closed its good eye.

Patsy stopped dead in her tracks. Maurice stood up slowly from where he had been crouching near his bed. Patsy's nose was in the air. She was sniffing. She slid one floppy paw forward, then another. Maurice sprang toward the bear, his arms outstretched.

"Don't lay a hand on that bear!" he cried.

It was too late. Patsy leaped. Over and down crashed the bear. All eight wheels of the roller skates spun in the air. Patsy sat on the bear and began to bay. Maurice could hear his mother, his father, and his uncle racing down the hall.

He ran to the window and flung it open. He grabbed a blanket from his bed and threw it over Patsy, who fell into a tangled heap alongside the bear. In a flash, Maurice had the bear up on its skates and on the sill. He gave it a shove and out it went through the window, the rope trailing behind it.

Mr. Klenk, who was sweeping the courtyard below and whistling softly to himself, heard the whir of spinning roller skates and looked up.

"Good grief!" he cried. "A giant penguin!"

"Whew!" said Maurice. "Safe this time."
Then he sank to the floor and smiled.

You can read more about Maurice and his collection in the book, Maurice's Room.

Questions

1. Why did Mr. Klenk think that he saw a giant penguin?

2. If Patsy could talk, what would she say about her visit to Maurice's room?

3. If you visited Maurice in his room, what question would you ask him? What do you think he would answer?

4. "Patsy sat on the bear and began to *bay*." What does *bay* mean in that sentence?
   a. Water with land on three sides.
   b. To bark or cry with a deep, long sound.
   c. To sniff something.

Activity

List six unusual things that you might find in Maurice's room. List things that are not in the story.

BOOKSHELF

Tuttle's Shell by Sal Murdocca. Lothrop, Lee & Shepard, 1976. Tuttle the Turtle has lost his shell! He and his friends begin a search to find it.

Miss Nelson Is Missing by Harry Allard and James Marshall. Houghton Mifflin, 1977. The children in Miss Nelson's class misbehave, and their teacher doesn't know what to do. Then one day a substitute teacher comes, and the children wish they had Miss Nelson back.

Warton and Morton by Russell E. Erickson. Lothrop, Lee & Shepard, 1976. Warton, a toad, and his brother Morton go camping, but are separated during a flood. As they try to find different ways home, they both have adventures.

Oh, What Nonsense! Collected by William Cole. Methuen, 1966. Here are fifty silly poems to make you smile and giggle.

2 Good Times

Stevie

Story and pictures by John Steptoe

Robert is the only child at his house until Stevie comes to stay. It's not long before Robert begins to feel that Stevie is a pest, as Robert will tell you in this story.

One day my momma told me, "You know you're gonna have a little friend come stay with you."

And I said, "Who is it?"

And she said, "You know my friend Mrs. Mack? Well, she has to work all week and I'm gonna keep her little boy."

I asked, "For how long?"

She said, "He'll stay all week and his mother will come pick him up on Saturdays."

The next day the doorbell rang. It was a lady and a kid. He was smaller than me. I ran to my mother. "Is that them?"

They went in the kitchen but I stayed out in the hall to listen.

The little boy's name was Steven but his mother kept calling him Stevie. My name is Robert but my momma don't call me Robertie.

And so Steve moved in, with his old crybaby self. He always had to have his way. And he was greedy too. Everything he sees he wants. "Could I have somma that? Gimme this." Man!

Since he was littler than me, while I went
to school he used to stay home and play
with my toys.

I used to get so mad at my mother when
I came home after school. "Momma, can't
you watch him and tell him to leave my stuff
alone?"

Then he used to like to get up on my bed
to look out the window and leave his dirty
footprints all over my bed. And my momma
never said nothin' to him.

I could never go anywhere without my
mother sayin' "Take Stevie with you now."

"But why I gotta take him everywhere I
go?" I'd say.

"Now if you were stayin' with someone
you wouldn't want them to treat you mean,"
my mother told me.

I had to take him out to play with me and my friends.

"Is that your brother, Bobby?" they'd ask me.

"No."

"Is that your cousin?"

"No! He's just my friend and he's stayin' at my house and my mother made me bring him."

"Ha, ha. You gotta baby-sit! Bobby the baby sitter!"

"Aw, be quiet. Come on, Steve. See! Why you gotta make all my friends laugh for?"

"Hey, come on, y'all, let's go play in the park. You comin', Bobby?" one of my friends said.

"Naw, my momma said he can't go in the park cause the last time he went he fell and hurt his knee, with his old stupid self."

And then they left.

"You see? You see! I can't even play with my friends. Man! Come on."

"I'm sorry, Robert. You don't like me, Robert? I'm sorry," Stevie said.

"Aw, be quiet. That's okay," I told him.

One time when my daddy was havin' company I was just sittin' behind the couch just listenin' to them talk and make jokes. And I wasn't makin' no noise. They didn't even know I was there!

Then here comes Stevie with his old loud self. Then when my father heard him, he yelled at *me* and told me to go upstairs.

Just cause of Stevie.

Sometimes people get on your nerves and they don't mean it or nothin' but they just bother you. Why I gotta put up with him? I used to have a lot of fun before he came to live with us.

One Saturday Steve's mother and father came to my house to pick him up like always. But they said that they were gonna move away and that Stevie wasn't gonna come back anymore.

So then he left. The next mornin' I got up to watch cartoons and I fixed two bowls of corn flakes. Then I just remembered that Stevie wasn't here.

Sometimes we had a lot of fun runnin' in and out of the house. Well, I guess my bed will stay clean from now on. But that wasn't so bad. He couldn't help it cause he was stupid.

I remember the time I ate the last piece of cake in the breadbox and blamed it on him.

I remember when I was doin' my homework I used to try to teach him what I had learned. He could write his name pretty good for his age.

I remember the time we hid under the covers with Daddy's flashlight.

We used to have some good times together.

I think he liked my momma better than his own, cause he used to call his mother "Mother" and he called my momma "Mommy."

Aw, no! I let my corn flakes get soggy thinkin' about him.

He was a nice little guy.

He was kinda like a little brother.

Little Stevie.

Questions

1. Tell about one *good* time and one *bad* time Robert had with Stevie.

2. How did Robert feel about Stevie at the end of the story?

3. If you asked Stevie how he liked staying with Robert, what might Stevie answer?

4. Which sentence says Stevie seemed *greedy?*
   a. "He plays with my toys."
   b. "Everything he sees he wants."
   c. "He could write his name."

Activity

Suppose that Stevie is going back to Robert's house for a day. List four things the boys might enjoy doing together.

Snoopy

Cartoons by Charles M. Schulz

87

From

Old Arthur

A story by Liesel Moak Skorpen

Pictures by Diane de Groat

For a long time Old Arthur worked on a
farm. He brought the cows home from the
fields and kept the fox from the hen house.
The day came, however, when Old Arthur
was too tired and too sleepy to do his jobs.
The farmer thought it was time to get rid of
Old Arthur. The old dog knew how the
farmer felt so he ran away to town.
There the dogcatcher found him and put him
in the animal shelter.

Most of the dogs in the animal shelter barked
when anyone opened the door.
But Old Arthur lay on the cold floor of his cage,
closed his old eyes,
and tried to go to sleep.
Sometimes someone stopped beside his cage,
shook his head slowly,
and walked away.
"People want puppies," the dogcatcher said.
"Nobody wants a mangy old mutt like that."

A little boy was standing by the cage.
He stood for a long time looking at Old Arthur,
pressing his face against the wire fence.
He didn't shake his head slowly.
He didn't walk away.
"Come here, William," his mother called.
"The puppies are over here."
"I don't want a puppy," William said.

The dogcatcher put his hand on William's shoulder.

"That dog is awful old," he said.

"He's not any good to anyone anymore.
Mind your mother,
and pick out one of the puppies."

"I don't want a puppy," William said.

"This is the one I want.
I like the way he looks at me.
I like the way he almost wags his tail."

William and his mother took Old Arthur home.

The first thing Old Arthur had
was a nice, warm bath.
Arthur had never had a bath before.
The soapsuds worried him a little,
but he was too tired to worry for long.
He closed his old eyes and fell fast asleep
while William was rubbing his back.

The next thing Arthur had
was a nice, warm supper
of milk and buttered toast.
William gave Old Arthur a bowl
with his name on the front
and his picture on the back.

William made a bed for Old Arthur
and put it beside his bed.
He lined the box with a clean, old quilt
to make it soft and warm.
That old dog had never slept in a bed before.
He had never even slept inside a house.
He felt a little lonely in his bed.
He tried to climb on William's bed,
but his legs were too old for jumping.
So William got down behind him
and gave him a little boost.

It was Old Arthur's job to wait for William
while William was at school.
That old dog was very good at waiting.
He had waited all his life.

It was Old Arthur's job to go for walks with William.
Nice, slow walks.
They took their time.
They didn't care about fast or far,
and they sat down a lot.
That old dog was good at sitting down.

It was Old Arthur's job to be "it"
for hide-and-seek.
William would hide in his closet
or under his bed.
Old Arthur didn't hunt very fast,
but he hunted very well.
Sometimes William made noises to help.
When Old Arthur found where William was hiding,
he licked him all over his face.

It was Old Arthur's job to lie on his back
while William rubbed his tum.
Old Arthur would wag his woolly tail
and make nice noises that William said were songs.

Wagging that woolly tail was the most important job
that that old dog did.
He wagged it for the baby
who lived in the crib upstairs.
He wagged it for the kittens
who lived in a box out back.
And he wagged it for the soft, gray rabbit
who lived in a wire hutch behind the house.

But his best wags were for William.

"What a good, old dog you are," William said.

"You're good for waiting

and walking

and sitting down

and for lying on your back and singing songs.

You're very good for playing hide-and-seek,

but what I like best is the way you wag your tail."

Then William would put his arms around Old Arthur,

and that old dog would wag that woolly tail

as fast as it would wag.

Questions

1. What did William like best about Old Arthur?

2. What do you think Old Arthur liked best about William?

3. Complete each sentence. Use a word from the story that starts with the same letter as each underlined word.

   a. Old Arthur was good for <u>waiting</u> and _____.

   b. A walk doesn't have to be <u>fast</u> or _____.

   c. Old Arthur <u>wagged</u> his _____ tail.

Activity

If you could have any pet in an animal shelter, what would you choose? Draw the animal's picture. Then write about it. Tell why you would choose this animal for a pet and what you might name it. What would you do to make your pet happy? What could it do to make *you* happy?

Learn About

Pictures in Books

Illustrators and Illustrations

When you choose a book, do you read the words or look at the pictures first? Many people like to turn the pages and look at the pictures. If they like the pictures, they may be interested in reading the words.

In a picture book the pictures help to tell the story. They show you how the people and the places look, and what is happening. The pictures also show the story's feeling, or *mood.* The pictures tell you if a story is funny, frightening, or sad. Pictures may help you catch the feeling of poems, too.

The people who make the pictures in a book are called *illustrators.* Each illustrator has a special way of creating pictures. On the next pages you will learn about three illustrators and their different ways of working.

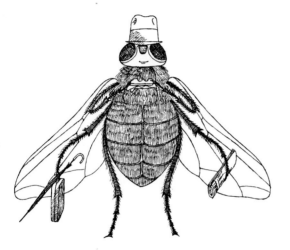

From the poem "The Fly in Rye"
by N. M. Bodecker

N. M. Bodecker likes to illustrate his
poems with unusual drawings. His poems make
you laugh, and his drawings—a fly, a cherry,
or a pickle dressed in clothing—are funny to see.

N. M. Bodecker's drawings show that
lines can do many things. See what thin lines
he used to show how light the fly's wings are.
Look at the short, thin lines he used to draw
the fly's fuzzy body and legs. For its eyes, he
used *crosshatching.* He made a set of lines
and then crossed them with another set.

From the story *Stevie*
by John Steptoe

The bold, heavy lines in this picture should catch your attention. Follow the lines around the picture. See how the lines form a circle that brings the mother and her son close together. John Steptoe, the author and illustrator, wants you to feel the love between mother and son. The picture, rather than the words, tells how they feel.

Notice how the bright colors in this picture may *overlap,* or flow one over the other. Look for the overlapping colors on the table.

This illustration was cut from a single piece of paper. Illustrations made this way are called *paper cuts.* Ed Young used this Chinese art form to illustrate *The Emperor and the Kite.* Paper cuts are made with tools that press straight down onto the paper to cut the shapes. Drops of dye are put on the paper to make the blended colors.

In this picture Ed Young helps you feel the excitement of the emperor climbing the rope. The emperor's robes fly out like wings. Imagine how hard it was to cut the emperor's robes.

From the Chinese folk tale *The Emperor and the Kite* retold by Jane Yolen

Now choose a story and illustrate your favorite part. Will you use crayon, paint, or cut paper? Try to catch the story's mood in your picture.

Amelia's Roller Coaster

From the story *Amelia's Flying Machine* by Barbara Shook Hazen

Pictures by Bert Dodson

A wonderful promise had been made to Amelia. Her father had promised to take her to the Chicago Fair for a roller coaster ride. She had to behave herself, though, and follow Grandma Otis's rules while her parents were away. Amelia was so excited about the roller coaster ride that she got her cousins, Katherine and Lucy, and her sister, Muriel, to help her build their own roller coaster. They constructed a wooden track leading from the barn window to the ground. They planned to come down the track in an orange crate fitted with roller skate wheels.

Trial Run

The next day, the roller coaster was ready to try out. Jimmy Watson, who lived on the neighboring farm, came over on his bike. He rode by the barn just as the girls were setting up the roller coaster.

"Not bad," said Jimmy when he saw it. "Not bad at all. But does it work? That's what I want to see."

"You will," said Amelia. "Just wait."

Jimmy leaned his bike against a tree. He sat down on the grass and watched. "Who's going to go first?" he asked.

"We could draw straws," said Amelia. "That would be fairest."

"No thanks," said Katherine. "Not me. You go first, Amelia."

"Yes, you first," said Lucy. "It was all your idea."

Muriel looked up at the track slanting out of the hayloft window and shuddered. "Not me, Meeley," she said. "It looks awfully high."

"See," Jimmy taunted. "Your sister is scared. Your cousins are scared. You're all scared to try it."

"Is that so?" said Amelia. "Well, I'm not scared. I'll gladly go first!"

Amelia tested the track to make sure it was firmly set on the ground. Then she picked up the roller coaster car. She carried it up the ladder to the hayloft and placed it on the wooden track. And then she squeezed herself inside the car. It was a tight fit.

She pushed herself part way out the barn window. She held on tight to the track sides and looked out. It was a long way down.

"What are you waiting for?" Jimmy called. "Are you scared?"

"Nope, not a bit!" said Amelia, letting go of the track sides.

The orange-crate car started to roll. It went faster and faster down the track. Amelia hugged her knees and held on tight. "Whee!" she cried. "I'm flying!"

The car gathered speed as it raced down the track. It hit the ground with a hard bump. It landed so hard that it flipped over.

Amelia flew out and fell on the ground. She lay on her stomach moaning, "Oooooooooooh!"

Katherine and Lucy and Muriel raced to her.

"Are you hurt?" asked Lucy, trying to see Amelia's face.

Even Jimmy looked worried. He held out a hand to help Amelia up. "Are you okay?" he asked.

"Sure. I'm okay," Amelia gasped. She turned herself over and brushed the dirt off her clothes.

Then she sat up and folded her arms. "I'm okay, all right," she said. "But the track isn't. The track is too short. That makes the slant too steep. And that's why the car hit the ground so hard.

"What we have to do," she said, getting up, "is add more boards and make the track longer."

"Why don't you just call it quits, huh?" suggested Jimmy.

"Not now!" said Amelia. "Not when I know what went wrong." She looked at Jimmy. "Come back this afternoon. You'll see how well it works."

Back to Work

Soon they were at it again. Amelia and Muriel laid the track on the ground. They added more boards until it was twice as long as before.

It was hard work, and it seemed even hotter than the day before. Katherine and Lucy went to the kitchen to make some lemonade.

Amelia ripped her stockings and Muriel got a splinter in her little finger. "Just a little longer," Amelia kept saying. "Just a few more boards."

They were almost done when Katherine and Lucy came back. "I hope Grandma Otis doesn't spoil everything," said Lucy. "She sounded suspicious. She wanted to know what we were up to."

"What did you tell her?" asked Amelia.

"The truth, of course," smiled Lucy. "I told her we were making lemonade and were going to take it out to you. Then I asked her if she wanted some. Then Grandma looked down her glasses and said, 'Young lady, I smell something fishy.' And I said, 'But, Grandma Otis, we haven't been near the river.'"

"And then we got out of there fast," said Katherine. She shook her head, "If Grandma decides to come out here, you're a goner."

"At least my trip to Chicago is," said Amelia.

A Second Try

When the lemonade was gone, the girls all helped to set up the track.

"It looks okay," said Amelia. "Let's just hope it works this time."

Soon Jimmy came back. "I wouldn't miss this for anything," he said with a grin.

Amelia made a face at him. Then she turned to the others. Once more she asked, "Shall we draw straws to see who goes first?"

"Not me," said Katherine. "Not after last time."

"Don't look at me," said Lucy.

Muriel shook her head. "Not me, Meeley," she said. "But if you go, I'll keep my fingers crossed."

"I knew it," said Jimmy. "You're too scared!"

Amelia stamped her foot. "That's not so," she said. "I'm not scared. Just you watch."

She climbed up to the hayloft and squeezed into the car. There she paused and took a deep breath. "It's got to work," she whispered to herself. "It's just got to."

"What are you waiting for?" teased Jimmy. "Santa Claus? Or me to try it for you?"

"Don't listen to him," yelled Lucy.

"Don't do it," said Katherine under her breath.

Muriel turned her head. She crossed as many fingers as she could. She closed her eyes tight. She didn't want to watch.

But she did want to see what was going on. When she opened her eyes to peek, she looked up and screamed, "Stop, Meeley! You can't go!"

The warning came too late. Amelia had
just let go. The car started to roll. As it
picked up speed, it went faster and faster
down the long track.

Amelia felt the speed and the slap of
wind in her face. "Wow! Look at me," she
shouted. "I'm really flying!"

The orange crate kept going. It rolled
to the end of the track, and then onto the
ground. Amelia waved and grinned at
Jimmy as she went by, and he grinned
back at her.

The car finally came to a stop—right by
a pair of black-stockinged feet.

"Oh-oh," gulped Amelia, looking up.

Grandmother Otis stared down at
Amelia. Her hands were on her hips. Her
eyebrows met in a disapproving *V*.

She spoke in her slow we'll-get-to-the-bottom-of-this voice. "Amelia Mary, what are you up to? And what kind of fool contraption is this? I suspected something. And I suspect your father will have something to say when he hears about it."

Grandmother Otis tapped her foot. "Young lady, was all this your idea?" she asked. "Or did somebody put you up to it?"

Amelia groaned. Telling the truth meant missing Chicago and the Fair and going with her father and everything.

"Yes, Gram," she said in a small voice. "It was all my idea." Then she sighed deeply.

Grandma Otis sighed, too. "Amelia Mary, I daresay I don't know whatever will become of you if you . . . "

"Ma'am," Jimmy interrupted, "it really wasn't Amelia's fault. I mean, she made it and rode on it. But I guess I kind of put her up to it."

Grandmother Otis turned toward Jimmy. She squinted through her glasses. "I might have thought so," she said. "I didn't think any granddaughter of mine could do such a foolhardy thing."

She shook her finger at Jimmy. "Yes, I should have known you were behind this, Jimmy Watson. You have a habit of getting into mischief. Why, I have half a mind . . ."

Amelia jumped to her feet. "No, Grandma! Jimmy's not to blame. I'm the one who . . ."

"I don't want to listen," said Grandma Otis sternly. She picked up her skirts. "Amelia. Muriel. Girls. Come with me," she ordered.

"As for you, young man"—she squinted hard at Jimmy—"you stay right here and take down this contraption. Right now. Break it up, every bit of it, mind you."

She turned on her heels and headed for the house.

Amelia hung back. "It isn't fair," she said to Jimmy. "You're getting the blame. It was my idea."

"So what!" Jimmy shrugged. "She'll get over it, and you'll get to go to Chicago. She never tells my pa, and she won't tell yours either."

"Know something?" Amelia smiled. "You're okay."

Jimmy grinned back. "Just send me a postcard with a picture of the roller coaster on it."

The Real Amelia

Amelia's full name was Amelia Earhart (EHR•hahrt). She grew up in the early 1900s, a time when the first airplanes were being flown. Not only did Amelia learn to fly, but she became one of the finest pilots of her time.

Amelia Earhart was the first woman to fly across the Atlantic Ocean alone. She received many honors for her solo flight, but she wanted to do something that no pilot had ever done. She wanted to fly around the world at the equator—a more difficult and dangerous route than any that had ever been flown.

In 1937 Amelia Earhart and her co-pilot Fred Noonan began their flight around the world. They made stops at South America, Africa, and India. Then they started across the Pacific Ocean. While looking for a tiny island in the Pacific where they were to refuel, they disappeared. They were never seen again. Nothing of their plane was ever found.

In a letter she left for her husband, Amelia Earhart had spoken about her flight. She had written, "I want to do it because I want to do it. Women must try to do things as men have tried. When they fail, their failures must be but a challenge to others."

Questions

1. Amelia said something that showed she was enjoying her ride on the roller coaster. What did she say?

2. Muriel screamed, "Stop, Meeley! You can't go!" Why did Muriel say that?

3. If Amelia had been afraid of Grandma Otis, what could she have said at the end of the story instead of "It was all my idea"?

4. Match a person in the story with one word that tells the most about that person.

   brave   fearful   suspicious   kind

Activity

Would you like Amelia as a friend? Give three reasons why Amelia would or would not make a good friend.

BOOKSHELF

Fish for Supper by M. B. Goffstein. Dial
Press, 1976. Grandmother spends every
day doing something that she enjoys very
much.

My Brother Fine with Me by Lucille Clifton.
Holt, Rinehart and Winston, 1975. Johnetta
decides to help her little brother run away.
But after he leaves, Johnetta begins to
worry about him.

His Mother's Dog by Liesel Moak Skorpen.
Harper & Row, 1978. A boy who has
always wanted a dog is upset when the
new puppy comes.

Angelita by Wendy Kesselman. Hill and
Wang, 1970. When Angelita and her
family move to New York, she misses the
sea and the mountains of Puerto Rico.

The 329th Friend by Marjorie Weinman
Sharmat. Four Winds Press, 1979. Though
Emery Raccoon invited 328 guests to
lunch, none of them have time to listen
to him.

3 Tell Me the Name

RUMPELSTILTSKIN

A German folk tale retold by Edith H. Tarcov

Pictures by Edward Gorey

PART ONE

Once upon a time there was a poor miller who had a beautiful daughter.

One morning, the king came riding by. He stopped to talk to the miller. The miller wanted to say something interesting. So he said: "King, I have a daughter—"

"I suppose she is beautiful," said the king.

"Oh, yes. She is beautiful," the miller said. "But she is more than that. My daughter . . . MY daughter . . . can spin straw into gold!"

"Spin straw into gold?" said the king. "Hm. Well! Tell your daughter to come to see me."

That evening the miller's daughter came to the king. The king took her into a little room. There was nothing in the room but

a heap of straw,

a chair,

and a spinning wheel.

"Now spin," said the king. "If you do not spin all this straw into gold by morning, you must die."

The king locked the door and went away.

Now the poor miller's daughter was all alone. She really did not know how to spin straw into gold. She did not know what to do. So she began to cry.

Suddenly the door opened, and a tiny little man came in.

"Good evening, miller's daughter," he said. "Why are you crying?"

"Oh!" she said. "Oh! The king told me to spin all this straw into gold. If it's not done by morning, I must die!"

"What will you give me if I do it for you?" the little man asked.

"I will give you my necklace," said the miller's daughter.

The little man took the necklace. Then he sat down at the spinning wheel.

Whirl! Whirl! Whirl! Three times he whirled the wheel and the work was done. Now that heap of straw was a heap of gold. And the little man went away.

As soon as the sun was up, the king came in. He looked at the heap of gold. The king was pleased.

"You have done well," he said to the miller's daughter. "But I need more gold than that."

That evening the king took the miller's
daughter into a bigger room. There was nothing
in that room but

> a chair,
>
> a spinning wheel,
>
> and a great big heap of straw.

"Now spin," said the king. "If you do not
spin all this straw into gold by morning, you
must die."

The king locked the door and went away.

Again the poor miller's daughter was all
alone. She looked at all that straw. She did not
know what to do. So she began to cry.

Again the door opened and the little man
came in.

"Good evening, miller's daughter," he said. "What will you give me if I spin all this straw into gold?"

"I will give you my ring," said the miller's daughter.

The little man took the ring. Then he sat down at the spinning wheel.

Whirl! Whirl! Whirl! Three times he whirled the wheel and the work was done. Now that great big heap of straw was a great big heap of gold. And the little man went away.

As soon as the sun was up, the king came in. He looked at that great big heap of gold. The king was pleased.

"You have done well," he said to the miller's daughter. "But I need more gold than that."

That evening the king took the miller's daughter into a very big room. There was nothing in that room but

>a chair,
>
>a spinning wheel,
>
>and heaps and heaps of straw!

"Now spin," said the king. "If you spin all this straw into gold by morning, you will be my wife."

The king locked the door and went away.

When the miller's daughter was all alone, the little man came again.

Again he said, "Good evening, miller's daughter. What will you give me if I spin all this straw into gold?"

"I have nothing left to give you," she said.

"Nothing?" the little man asked.

"Nothing," said the miller's daughter.

"I will help you," said the little man. "But you must promise to give me something. . . . "

"Anything! Anything you ask!" she cried.

"Then promise me," the little man said. "Promise me that when you are queen you will give me your first baby."

"Yes! Yes! I promise!" said the miller's daughter. And she thought, Who knows if I really shall be queen? And if I am queen, who knows if I shall have a baby? "Yes! Yes!" she said again. "I promise!"

The little man sat down at the spinning wheel.

Whirl! Whirl! Whirl! Three times he whirled the wheel and the work was done. Now those heaps and heaps of straw were heaps and heaps of gold. And the little man went away.

As soon as the sun was up the king came in. He looked at the heaps and heaps of gold. The king was very pleased.

"My dear," said the king. "We will be married this very day!"

And so the miller's daughter became queen.

A year later, the king and queen had a beautiful baby.

PART TWO

One evening the queen was in her room, playing with her baby. Suddenly, the little man came into the room.

"Good evening, queen," he said. "Now give me what you promised."

The queen had forgotten the little man. She had forgotten her promise, too.

"What promise?" she asked.

"You promised to give me your first baby," said the little man.

"I cannot give you my baby," said the queen. "You may have all the riches of the kingdom, but let me keep my baby."

"No, queen," said the little man. "A baby is dearer to me than all the riches of the world."

The queen began to cry. She cried so hard that the little man felt sorry for her.

"I will give you three days," he said. "If in three days you know my name, you may keep your baby. I will come every evening, for three evenings. Each time I will ask if you know my name."

And the little man went away.

The next morning the queen called for her messenger. "Messenger," she said. "Go through the town. Find out all the names people have. Come back before evening and tell them all to me."

That evening the little man came into the queen's room.

"Good evening, queen," he said. "Do you know my name?"

"Is it Al?" she asked.

"No," said the little man. "That's not my name."

"Is it Bill?"

"No."

"Is it Charlie?"

"No."

So they went, on and on and on. But all the little man said was: "No. No, no. That's not my name."

That very evening, as soon as the little man had gone away, the queen called for her messenger.

"Messenger," she said. "Go through the kingdom. Find out all the strange names people have. Come back tomorrow, before evening, and tell them all to me. Hurry."

On the second evening the little man came into the queen's room.

"Good evening, queen," he said. "Do you know my name?"

The queen asked him all the strange names her messenger had found.

"Is it Angel Face?" she asked.

"No," said the little man. "That's not my name."

"Is it Bump-on-a-Lump?"

"No."

"Is it Diddle Dump?"

"No."

So they went, on and on and on. But all the little man said was: "No. No, no. That's not my name."

That evening, as soon as the little man had gone away, the queen called for her messenger.

"Messenger," she said. "Go once more through the kingdom. You must find more names for me! Come back tomorrow, before evening, and tell them all to me. Hurry!"

On the third day, it was almost evening when the messenger came back.

"I could not find any new names for you," he said.

"Not any new names at all?" asked the queen.

"Well," said the messenger. "I did find something. Something very strange . . . "

"Tell me," said the queen. "And hurry!"

"Last night," he said, "I went up high, high into the mountains. I went deep into the woods. There I saw a little house. In front of that little house there was a fire. And around that little fire a tiny man was dancing. While he was dancing, he was singing:

Tonight my cakes I bake.
Tonight my brew I make.
Tomorrow, tomorrow, tomorrow
The queen's little baby I take!
Lucky I'll go as lucky I came
For RUMPELSTILTSKIN is my name!"

How happy the queen was to hear that name!

Now it was the third evening, and the little man came again.

"Good evening, queen," he said. "Do you know my name?"

"Tell me, is it Tom?" the queen asked.

"No."

"Hm . . . let me see. Is it Dick?"

"No."

"Well, let me think . . . . Is it Harry?"

"No." The little man laughed and he shook his head. "No, no. That's not my name."

"Then . . . tell me . . . " asked the queen. "Could it be . . . ? Is it . . . RUMPELSTILTSKIN?"

How angry the little man was! He stamped so hard with his right foot that he made a deep hole in the floor.

Oh, he was angry! He stamped hard with his left foot, too. And he fell deep into the earth.

No one has seen him since.

Questions

1. *Three* things happen *three* times in the story. What is *one* of those things?

2. The miller's daughter had two big problems. What were they?

3. What work does a *miller* do?
   a. weaves cloth   b. grinds grain
           c. drives horses

Activity

I don't think the Queen played fair.

She did what she had to do. She didn't want to lose her life or her baby.

Draw yourself. Write what you would say about the Queen and what she did.

I Am Rose

From a poem by Gertrude Stein

I am Rose my eyes are blue
I am Rose and who are you?
I am Rose and when I sing
I am Rose like anything.

146

Pictures by Susan Jaekel

Pudden Tame

A folk rhyme

What's your name?
　　Pudden Tame.
What's your other?
　　Bread and Butter.
Where do you live?
　　In a sieve.
What's your number?
　　Cucumber.

From

Rufus M.

A story by Eleanor Estes
Pictures by Susan Lexa

Rufus Moffat wanted a book. His older brother and his sisters were reading library books, but they said he was too young. Besides, he couldn't even read yet. That made Rufus mad. He knew how to get to the library by himself. He even knew where to find one of the Brownie books he liked. Reading? It was easy. Flipping pages. He could do that. It would be just as easy to take a book out of the library. So Rufus went to the library, chose his book, and handed it to the lady behind the desk.

"Do you have a card?" the lady asked.

Rufus felt in his pockets. Sometimes he carried around an old playing card or two. Today he didn't have one.

"No," he said.

"You'll have to have a card to get a book."

"I'll go and get one," said Rufus.

The lady put down her cards. "I mean a library card," she explained kindly. "It looks to me as though you are too little to have a library card. Do you have one?"

"No," said Rufus. "I'd like to though."

"I'm afraid you're too little," said the lady. "You have to write your name to get one. Can you do that?"

Rufus nodded his head confidently. Writing. Lines up and down. He'd seen that done. And the letters that Mama had tied in bundles in the closet under the stairs were covered with writing. Of course he could write.

"Well, let's see your hands," said the lady.

Rufus obligingly showed this lady his hands, but she did not like the look of them. She cringed and clasped her head as though the sight hurt her.

"Oh," she gasped. "You'll just have to go home and wash them before we can even think about joining the library and borrowing books."

This was a complication upon which
Rufus had not reckoned. However, all it
meant was a slight delay. He'd wash his
hands and then he'd get the book. He
turned and went out of the library, found his
scooter safe among the Christmas trees, and
pushed it home. He surprised Mama by
asking to have his hands washed. When this
was done, he mounted his scooter again and
returned all the long way to the library. It
was not just a little trip to the library. It was
a long one. A long one and a hot one on a
day like this. But he didn't notice that. All he
was bent on was getting his book and taking
it home and reading with the others on the
front porch. They were all still there,
brushing flies away and reading.

Again Rufus hid his scooter in the pine trees, encircled the light, and went in.

"Hello," he said.

"Well," said the lady. "How are they now?"

Rufus had forgotten he had had to wash his hands. He thought she was referring to the other Moffats. "Fine," he said.

"Let me see them," she said, and she held up her hands.

Oh! His hands! Well, they were all right, thought Rufus, for Mama had just washed them. He showed them to the lady. There was a silence while she studied them. Then she shook her head. She still did not like them.

"Ts, ts, ts!" she said. "They'll have to be cleaner than that."

Rufus looked at his hands. Supposing he went all the way home and washed them again, she still might not like them. However, if that is what she wanted, he would have to do that before he could get the Brownie book . . . and he started for the door.

"Well now, let's see what we can do," said the lady. "I know what," she said. "It's against the rules but perhaps we can wash them in here." And she led Rufus into a little room that smelled of paste where lots of new books and old books were stacked up. In one corner was a little round sink and Rufus washed his hands again. Then they returned to the desk. The lady got a chair and put a newspaper on it. She made Rufus stand on this because he was not big enough to write at the desk otherwise.

Then the lady put a piece of paper covered with a lot of printing in front of Rufus, dipped a pen in the ink well and gave it to him.

"All right," she said. "Here's your application. Write your name here."

All the writing Rufus had ever done before had been on big pieces of brown wrapping paper with lots of room on them. Rufus had often covered those great sheets of paper with his own kind of writing at home. Lines up and down.

But on this paper there wasn't much space. It was already covered with writing. However, there was a tiny little empty space and that was where Rufus must write his name, the lady said. So, little space or not, Rufus confidently grasped the pen with his left hand and dug it into the paper. He was not accustomed to pens, having always worked with pencils until now, and he made a great many holes and blots and scratches.

"Gracious," said the lady. "Don't bear down so hard! And why don't you hold it in your right hand?" she asked, moving the pen back into his right hand.

Rufus started again scraping his lines up and down and all over the page, this time using his right hand. Wherever there was an empty space he wrote. He even wrote over some of the print for good measure. Then he waited for the lady, who had gone off to get a book for some man, to come back and look.

"Oh," she said as she settled herself in her swivel chair, "is that the way you write? Well . . . it's nice, but what does it say?"

"Says Rufus Moffat. My name."

Apparently these lines up and down did not spell Rufus Moffat to this lady. She shook her head.

"It's nice," she repeated. "Very nice. But nobody but you knows what it says. You have to learn to write your name better than that before you can join the library."

Rufus was silent. He had come to the library all by himself, gone back home to wash his hands, and come back because he wanted to take books home and read them the way the others did. He had worked hard. He did not like to think he might have to go home without a book.

The library lady looked at him a moment and then she said quickly before he could get himself all the way off the big chair, "Maybe you can *print* your name."

Rufus looked at her hopefully. He thought
he could write better than he could print, for
his writing certainly looked to him exactly
like all grown people's writing. Still he'd try
to print if that was what she wanted.

The lady printed some letters on the top
of a piece of paper. "There," she said.
"That's your name. Copy it ten times and
then we'll try it on another application."

Rufus worked hard. He worked so hard
the knuckles showed white on his brown fist.

He worked for a long, long time, now with his right hand and now with his left. Sometimes a boy or a girl came in, looked over his shoulder and watched, but he paid no attention. From time to time the lady studied his work and she said, "That's fine. That's fine." At last she said, "Well, maybe now we can try." And she gave him another application.

All Rufus could get, with his large generous letters, in that tiny little space where he was supposed to print his name, was R-U-F. The other letters he scattered here and there on the card. The lady did not like this either. She gave him still another blank. Rufus tried to print smaller and this time he got RUFUS in the space, and also he crowded an M at the end. Since he was doing so well now the lady herself printed the *offat* part of Moffat on the next line.

"This will have to do," she said. "Now take this home and ask your mother to sign it on the other side. Bring it back on Thursday and you'll get your card."

Rufus's face was shiny and streaked with dirt where he had rubbed it. He never knew there was all this work to getting a book. The other Moffats just came in and got books. Well, maybe they had had to do this once too.

Rufus held his hard-earned application in one hand and steered his scooter with the other. When he reached home Joey, Jane and Sylvie were not around any longer. Mama signed his card for him, saying, "My! So you've learned how to write!"

"Print," corrected Rufus.

Mama kissed Rufus and he went back out. The lady had said to come back on Thursday, but he wanted a book today. When the other Moffats came home, he'd be sitting on the top step of the porch, reading. That would surprise them. He smiled to himself as he made his way to the library for the third time.

When he reached home, he showed Mama his book. She smiled at him, and gave his cheek a pat. She thought it was fine that he had gone to the library and joined all by himself and taken out a book. And she thought it was fine when Rufus sat down at the kitchen table, was busy and quiet for a long, long time, and then showed her what he had done.

He had printed RUFUS M. That was what he had done. And that's the way he learned to sign his name. And that's the way he always did sign his name for a long, long time.

Questions

1. What did a *card* mean to Rufus?

2. What did a *card* mean to the librarian?

3. Rufus had several problems in this story. Tell about one of those problems and how Rufus solved it.

4. Rufus learned to *print* his name. Which answer shows what he did?

   a. *Rufus M.*   b. Rufus M,

   c. *Mm*

Activity

Rufus has a library card now. He wants to get some books from the library. Make a list of five books you think Rufus would like. Write the author's name after each book title.

About ELEANOR ESTES

Though she always wanted to become a writer, Eleanor Estes (EHS•teez) said, "I never really decided to write for children. It just happened that I did." She has filled her warm and funny stories with many memories of her own childhood. Often, in the middle of the night, she would remember what someone said or did. She wrote these memories down, and later used them in the stories she wrote.

Eleanor Estes grew up in West Haven, Connecticut. After graduating from high school, she worked as a librarian. When her first book, *The Moffats,* was published, she decided to become a full-time writer. Several of her books are about the adventures of the Moffat family.

More Books by Eleanor Estes

The Hundred Dresses
The Middle Moffat
Ginger Pye

Paper Boats

A poem by Rabindranath Tagore

Day by day I float my paper boats one by one down
 the running stream.
In big black letters I write my name on them and
 the name of the village where I live.
I hope that someone in some strange land will
 find them and know who I am.
I load my little boats with *shiuli* flowers from
 our garden, and hope that these blooms of dawn
 will be carried safely to land in the night.
I launch my paper boats and look up into the sky
 and see the little clouds setting their white
 bulging sails.
I know not what playmate of mine in the sky sends
 them down the air to race with my boats!
When night comes I bury my face in my arms and
 dream that my paper boats float on and on
 under the midnight stars.
The fairies of sleep are sailing in them, and the
 lading is their baskets full of dreams.

Picture by Christa Kieffer

165

Oliphaunt

A poem by J. R. R. Tolkien

Gray as a mouse,
Big as a house,
Nose like a snake,
I make the earth shake,
As I tramp through the grass;
Trees crack as I pass.
With horns in my mouth
I walk in the South,
Flapping big ears.
Beyond count of years
I stump round and round,
Never lie on the ground,
Not even to die.
Oliphaunt am I,
Biggest of all,
Huge, old, and tall.
If ever you'd met me,
You wouldn't forget me.
If you never do,
You won't think I'm true;
But old Oliphaunt am I,
And I never lie.

Picture by Sharon Harker

BOOKSHELF

Fish Is Fish by Leo Lionni. Pantheon, 1970. Leaving his friend fish in a pond, frog travels on land to see new sights. When frog returns, fish wants to get out of the pond to see the world, too.

Crow Boy by Taro Yashima. Viking Press, 1955. A shy boy has a difficult time making friends in school until his classmates learn about his remarkable talent.

Me and Neesie by Eloise Greenfield. T. Y. Crowell, 1975. Neesie is a make-believe friend who tells Janell what to do. When Janell's Aunt Bea visits, trouble starts for Neesie.

The Hundred Dresses by Eleanor Estes. Harcourt Brace & World, 1944. Girls at school don't believe Wanda when she says she has a hundred dresses at home.

Thumbelina by Hans Christian Andersen. Dial Press, 1979. A girl no bigger than your thumb is named Thumbelina. Though small, she has many big adventures.

4 You Can't Catch Me

The Cat Came Back

A folk song adapted by Dahlov Ipcar

There was an old yellow cat
    had troubles all her own.
No one seemed to want her,
    but she wouldn't leave her home.
They tried everything they knew
    to drive that cat away.
They took her to Alaska,
    and they told her for to stay—

BUT

The cat came back,
She couldn't stay no longer.
The cat came back,
'Cause she couldn't stay away.
The cat came back,
We thought she was a goner,
But the cat came back

ON THE VERY NEXT DAY!

171

The cat she had some kittens
    and a family of her own,
Seven little kittens,
    when there came a cyclone.
Tore the houses all apart
    and tossed the cat around,
Though the air was full of kittens,
    not a one was ever found—

BUT

The cat came back,
She couldn't stay no longer.
The cat came back,
'Cause she couldn't stay away.
The cat came back,
We thought she was a goner,
But the cat came back

ON THE VERY NEXT DAY!

Then they took her to Cape Canaveral
    and found that cat a place
Right inside a rocket
    that was heading into space.
They thought that when she reached the moon,
    they'd really have it made,
But the cat returned in triumph
    for a ticker tape parade!

Oh, the cat came back!
She couldn't stay no longer.
The cat came back,
'Cause she couldn't stay away.
The cat came back,
We thought she was a goner,
But the cat came back

ON THE VERY NEXT DAY!

Dance of the Animals

A play adapted from a Puerto Rican folk tale retold by Pura Belpré
Pictures by Willi K. Baum

Glossary of Spanish Words

amiga mía (ah•MEE•gah MEE•ah) My friend.
amigo (ah•MEE•goh) Friend.
buenos días (BWAY•nohs THEE•ahs) Good day.
gracias (GRAH•see•ahs) Thank you.
hola (OH•lah) Hello.
jotas (HOH•tahs) Traditional Spanish dances.
señor (sen•YOHR) Sir, mister.
señora (sen•YOHR•ah) Lady, madam.
sí (SEE) Yes.

Characters

Narrator 1   Señor Lion   Señor Dog

Narrator 2   Señora Lioness   Señora Dog

Narrator 3   Señora Mare   Señor Goat

Narrator 4   Señora Donkey

Setting: In the forest.

SCENE ONE

Narrator 1: Once upon a time, a lion and a lioness lived together near a great forest. Among their neighbors were Señor Horse and Señora Mare, Señor and Señora Donkey, Señor Bull and Señora Cow, Señor and Señora Dog, and Señor and Señora Goat.

Times were hard for Señor Lion and Señora Lioness, and soon the day came when they faced each other with nothing to fix for a meal.

Señora Lioness: We must do something. If times keep up like this, we shall certainly die. We cannot let that happen, for are we not the strongest beasts in the forest? Has it not been said that the bigger fish shall eat the smaller?

Señor Lion: True enough. Something must be done.

Narrator 1: Señor Lion set to thinking for a while. A short time later, an idea came to him.

Señor Lion: I have it. And a splendid idea it is, even if I have to say it myself. Listen. Which meat do we like the best?

Señora Lioness: Goat's meat.

Señor Lion: Right. It is the finest, the juiciest and certainly the tastiest. Ah, *Señora mía,* you shall see.

Señora Lioness: But how are we going to get such fresh and delicious meat?

Señor Lion: I will tell you. Listen carefully. We shall give a ball—a grand ball. And we shall invite our friends to come to it. You, who are so well liked, will ask our neighbors, and they will not refuse. We will build a roasting pit. Everyone will be dancing. And when the goats get close to the pit, I will push them into the hot coals. The rest depends on me. How do you like my plan?

Narrator 1: Señora Lioness thought for a while, at first shaking her head slowly as if the plan did not meet with her approval. Then suddenly she realized what it meant.

Señora Lioness: What a good idea! Meat at last.

Señor Lion: You will have to hurry if my plans are to be carried out.

Narrator 1: Señora Lioness went out to invite the neighbors, while Señor Lion stayed home to prepare for the big affair.

Scene Two

Señora Lioness: *Hola!* Señora Mare!

Señora Mare: *Hola!* Señora Lioness. What are you doing around these parts, my good friend?

Señora Lioness: I came to invite you to a dance. You and Señor Horse have such fine long legs and such strong hoofs. We need you for our orchestra. Could you not come and play the drum?

Señora Mare: Oh, most certainly. Only yesterday was I saying that we needed a little recreation. Yes, we will come and play the drum.

Señora Lioness: *Gracias.*

Narrator 2: And Señora Lioness went on her way. Pretty soon she found Señora Donkey.

Señora Lioness: Ah, *amiga mía.* I was coming to see you. We are giving a ball and would like to have you and Señor Donkey come. Señor Horse and Señora Mare are coming to play the drum. Won't you and Señor Donkey come and play the trombone?

Señora Donkey: Why, yes, Señora Lioness, we will be there without fail.

Señora Lioness: *Gracias, gracias.*

Narrator 2: On went Señora Lioness, faster and faster as she felt the pangs of hunger in her empty stomach. She had not had goat's meat in such a long time. She crossed lane after lane inviting more and more neighbors. She gave each invitation with such graciousness that those invited felt that the dance would not be a success unless they accepted.

Señora Lioness found Señor and Señora Dog sitting under the shade of a great tree. She greeted them a little breathless, for she had walked quite a distance now.

Señora Lioness: *Hola, amigos.* There is a great ball at our place tonight. You must both come.

Señor Dog: I will go, but Señora Dog stays home.

Señora Dog: I will go, too.

Señor Dog: No! No!

Señora Dog: *Sí! Sí!*

Señora Lioness: Oh, my friends, I must leave you to decide the matter yourselves. I must call on Señor Goat.

Señor Dog: Wait, Señora Lioness. Señor Goat is my best friend. I will take you to him.

Narrator 2: Once at Señor Goat's place, Señor Dog took him aside and suggested that he go alone to the dance. Señor Goat agreed.

Señor Dog: Señora Lioness, thank you for your kind invitation. Señor Goat and I will gladly come. The Señoras, however, will stay home.

Narrator 2: Señora Lioness left with a sad heart, for Señor Goat would not provide enough meat for two.

Señora Lioness (*To herself*): Oh, what will Señor Lion say when he learns that only Señor Goat is coming? Señor Goat is so small and thin.

SCENE THREE

Narrator 3: Señora Lioness soon reached home.
Señor Lion had dug a roasting pit in which hot
coals burned brightly.

Señor Lion: Well, you are here at last. Are they all
coming?

Señora Lioness: Yes, all—that is, except. . . .

Narrator 3: Señora Lioness never finished the
sentence, for so excited was Señor Lion that
he danced for joy and then went to tend the
fire. Señora Lioness had hardly finished putting
on her garland of flowers when the first guests
arrived.

Señor Lion: *Buenos días,* Señor and Señora Donkey.

Señora Donkey: What a beautiful garland! And how becoming.

Señora Lioness: *Gracias,* my friend.

Narrator 3: More guests arrived, all clean and looking their very best. Señora Cat had woven a bunch of honeysuckle on a blue ribbon around her neck. Señor Bull and Señora Cow had threaded grey and red wreaths around their horns. Last came Señor Dog and Señor Goat. Señor Lion greeted them.

Señor Lion: And where are the Señoras? Aren't they coming?

Señor Goat: No.

Señor Dog: Oh, no.

Narrator 3: Señor Lion leaned over and whispered to his wife.

Señor Lion: My dear, we shall have to eat them both, since Señora Goat did not come.

Narrator 3: Señor Lion and Señora Lioness opened
the dance. The couples whirled, stamped, and
bellowed. What tangos and *jotas!* Waltzes
mixed with mazurkas and traditional dances.

What a mixture of sounds! Señor Dog
barked and howled. Señor and Señora Cat
meowed, while the constant stamping of Señor
Donkey and the brays of Señora Mare filled the
place.

Suddenly on one of the turns of the dance
Señor Goat and Señor Dog spied the fire
in the pit.

Señor Goat: *Amigo*, I do not like the look of that fire. Let us go, for this fire is meant for us. No doubt, Señor Lion means to eat us.

Narrator 3: Then, through the dancers they pulled and pushed, skipping all the time until they reached the woods.

Señor Dog: Hurry, *amigo!* Now we must run just as fast as we possibly can.

Narrator 3: Meanwhile, at the ball things went on as before. Suddenly Señor Lion missed Señor Dog and Señor Goat. As quickly as he could without causing suspicion, he left and followed Señor Dog's and Señor Goat's trail.

SCENE FOUR

Narrator 4: The afternoon was cool and the air was heavy with the scent of the acacia trees in full bloom. The wind began to blow and with it came rain, slowly at first and then in great torrents. The river soon was swollen with the sudden downpour.

Señor Dog: *Amigo,* I am going to swim across the river. Come! Follow me.

Señor Goat (*To himself, as he stands by the bank of the river*): Señor Lion will soon be here and I cannot swim. Oh, for a good safe hiding place! Ah, perhaps I can hide in that stack of hay.

Narrator 4: No sooner had Señor Goat hidden himself and Señor Dog made his way across the river, than Señor Lion appeared. On the other side of the river, Señor Dog stood, happily jumping around and mocking Señor Lion.

Señor Lion (*Picking up and throwing a large stone*): Watch out, Señor Dog!

Señor Dog: Oh, my friend, see that bundle of straw near you? Why don't you try to throw a piece of that at me?

Señor Lion: One piece, indeed. I will throw the whole stack at you.

Narrator 4: And Señor Lion leaned forward and tried to pick up the heavy bundle of hay. But he only slipped and fell on his back. At this Señor Dog leaped up and barked for joy.

Señor Dog: Try again, my friend.

Narrator 4: Señor Lion got up and tugged at the straw bundle again. He pulled and pulled and finally managed to lift it and hurl it across the river. No sooner did it land on the ground than Señor Goat jumped out of his hiding place. And accompanied by Señor Dog, he began to leap joyfully in the air.

Señor Goat: Señor Lion, thanks for helping me over. If I did lose most of my tail, my life, indeed, I saved.

Narrator 4: Señor Lion's rage had no limit and, looking down at his paws, he discovered that he had a large amount of fur entangled in his claws. Then he laughed.

Señor Lion: So you have, my friend, but by your stump you'll tell your tale.

Narrator 4: And it is true, because even to this day most goats have only a stump for a tail.

Questions

Here are riddles about the animals in *Dance of the Animals.* Guess who each one is.

1. I did not go to the dance. I'm glad now because I can't swim.

2. Everyone likes me, and I like others— especially goats!

3. I thought that the dance might be dangerous!

4. My tail tells the tale.

Activity

Make up a riddle about a *character* (KAR•ik•tuhr)—a person or an animal in a story or a play. Write two or more clues. The clues might tell what the character did or said, or how the character feels about someone in the story.

About PURA BELPRÉ

For a long time, folk tales
all over the world have been
passed down by storytellers.
A storyteller of our own time
is Pura Belpré (PAW•rah
BEL•pray), who tells the folk
tales she heard as a child in
Puerto Rico.

While working in the New
York Public Library, Pura
Belpré told folk tales to
children. To make her stories
more lively, she began making and using puppets.
When people wanted to read the folk tales, Pura
Belpré wrote them down. Though many of the
stories are in books now, she still likes to tell the
tales with her handmade puppets.

More Books by Pura Belpré

The Rainbow-Colored Horse
Perez and Martina
The Tiger and the Rabbit

The Emperor and the Kite

A Chinese folk tale retold by Jane Yolen
Pictures by Ed Young

*The ancient sport of kite flying began
long ago in China. No one knows for certain
when or where in China kites were invented,
and no one knows who flew the first one.*

*Kites are found in many old Chinese folk
tales. In this folk tale, a stick-and-paper kite
is the favorite toy of a lonely Emperor's
daughter named Djeow Seow (jeeOH seeOW).*

Once in ancient China there lived a
princess who was the fourth daughter of the
emperor. She was very tiny. In fact she was
so tiny her name was Djeow Seow, which
means "the smallest one." And, because she
was so tiny, she was not thought very
much of—when she was thought of at all.

Her brothers, who were all older and bigger and stronger than she, were thought of all the time. And they were like four rising suns in the eyes of their father.

Her three sisters were all older and bigger and stronger than she. They were like three midnight moons in the eyes of their father.

But Djeow Seow was like a tiny star in the emperor's sight. The emperor often forgot he had a fourth daughter at all.

Every morning, when the wind came from the east past the rising sun, Djeow Seow flew her kite. And every evening, when the wind went to the west past the setting sun, she flew her kite. Her toy was like a flower in the sky.

A monk who passed the palace every day made up a poem about her kite.

> *My kite sails upward,*
> *Mounting to the high heavens.*
> *My soul goes on wings.*

Each day Princess Djeow Seow thanked him for his poem. Then she went back to flying her kite.

But just as the wind is not always peaceful, all was not peaceful in the kingdom. There were evil men plotting against the emperor. They crept up on him one day when he was alone. Only Princess Djeow Seow saw what happened.

The evil men took the emperor to a tower in the middle of a wide, treeless plain. The tower had only a single window. The men sealed the door with bricks and mortar. Then they rode back to the palace and said that the emperor was dead.

When his sons and daughters heard this, they ran away. But Djeow Seow built a hut of twigs and branches at the edge of the plain.

Every day at dawn and again at dark, she would walk across the plain to the tower. And there she would sail her stick-and-paper kite. To the kite string she tied a tiny basket filled with rice and poppyseed cakes, water chestnuts and green tea. The kite pulled the basket high, high in the air, up as high as the window in the tower. And, in this way, she kept her father alive.

So they lived for many days.

The evil men were cruel, and the people of the country were very sad.

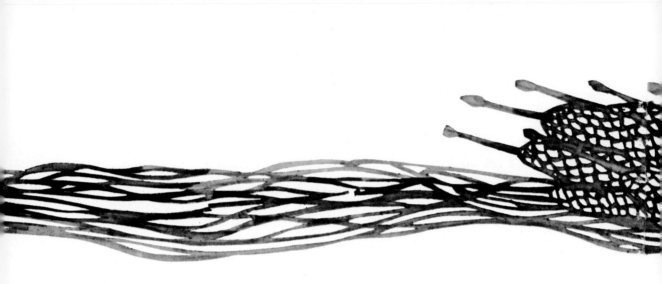

One day, as the princess prepared a basket of food for her father, the old monk passed by her hut. She smiled at him, but he seemed not to see her.

Yet, as he passed, he repeated his poem in a loud voice. He said:

> *My kite sails upward,*
> *Mounting to the high heavens.*
> *My emperor goes on wings.*

The princess started to thank him. But then she stopped. Something was different. The words were not quite right.

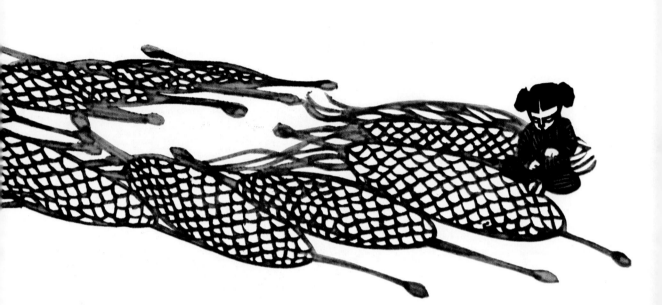

And then Djeow Seow understood. The monk was telling her something important.

Each day after that, Djeow Seow was busy. She twined a string of grass and vines, and wove in strands of her own long black hair. When her rope was as thick as her waist and as high as the tower, she was ready. She attached the rope to the string of the stick-and-paper kite, and made her way across the treeless plain.

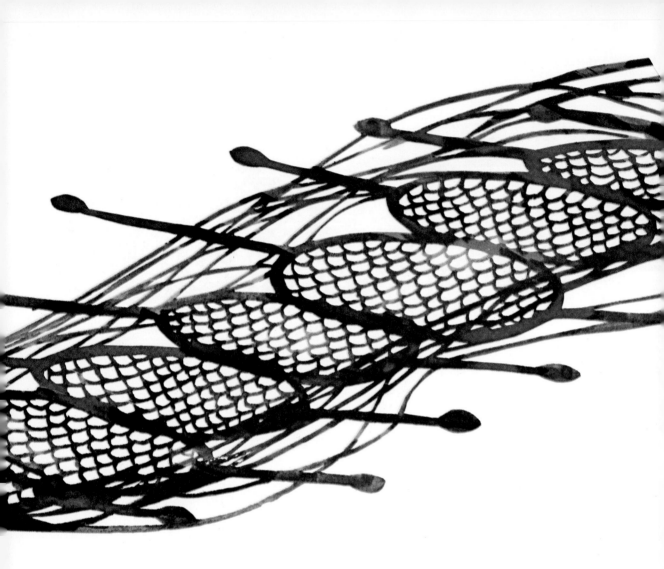

When she reached the tower, she called
to her father. But her voice was as tiny as
she, and her words were lost in the wind.

At last, though, the emperor looked out
and saw his daughter flying her kite. He
expected the tiny basket of food to sail up
to his window as it had done each day. But
what should he see but the strand of vines
and grass and long black hair. The wind
was raging above, holding the kite in its
steely grip. And the princess was below,
holding tight to the end of the rope.

The emperor leaned out of the tower
window and grasped the heavy strand. He
brought it into his tower room and
loosened the string of the kite. He set the
kite free.

Then the emperor tied one end of the thick strand to the heavy iron bar across the window, and the other end stretched all the way down to Djeow Seow's tiny hands.

The emperor stepped to the window sill and slid down the rope. His robes billowed out around him like the wings of a bright kite.

When his feet reached the ground, he knelt before his tiny daughter. And he touched the ground before her with his lips. Then he rose and embraced her, and she almost disappeared in his arms.

He lifted the tiny princess to his shoulders and carried her all the way back to the palace.

At the palace, the emperor was greeted
by wild and cheering crowds. The people
were tired of the evil men, but they had
been afraid to act. With the emperor once
again to guide them, they threw the evil
men into prison.

And when the other sons and daughters
of the emperor heard of his return, they
hurried home to welcome their father.
When they arrived, they were surprised to
find Djeow Seow on a tiny throne by their
father's side.

To the end of his days, the emperor
ruled with Princess Djeow Seow close by.

And, too, it is said that Djeow Seow
ruled after him, as gentle as the wind and,
in her loyalty, as unyielding.

Questions

1. Who were like four rising suns?

2. Who was like the gentle, unyielding wind?

3. What was like a flower in the sky?

4. Choose the word the author used instead of each underlined word.

         evil   twined   ancient

   a. Djeow Seow lived in <u>long-ago</u> China.
   b. <u>Bad</u> men put the emperor in a tower.
   c. Djeow Seow <u>made</u> a string of grass and vines.

Activity

Djeow Seow needs a kite to fly when she is ruling the country. Draw a beautiful kite for her. Then complete the sentences to tell about the kite. Compare it to something beautiful.

The kite will look like a _____.

The kite will fly like a _____.

About ED YOUNG

Do you ever daydream? When Ed Young was a boy in China, he daydreamed so much that his mother wondered what would become of him. The rest of the family, however, enjoyed the plays and the drawings Ed Young made up from his dreams.

Ed Young came to the United States to go to art school. *The Mean Mouse and Other Mean Stories* was the first book he illustrated. Since then, he has become well known as an illustrator who uses modern forms of ancient arts. In *The Emperor and the Kite,* he used the Chinese art of paper cutting.

More Books Illustrated by Ed Young

The Yellow Boat
Chinese Mother Goose Rhymes
The Girl Who Loved the Wind

Great Escapes

Peter and the Wolf *by Sergei Prokofiev*

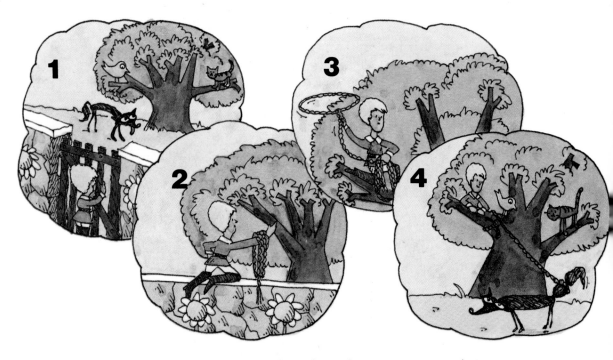

In some stories the characters get into trouble. They need a way to get out of that trouble. They need a "great escape" plan. Sometimes the characters think of their own "great escape" plans. Sometimes someone else helps them escape. In the story above, who helps the cat and the bird escape from the wolf?

The characters in the stories below all had "great escape" plans. Choose one or both of these stories. Tell what the plans were by answering the questions.

1. **Dance of the Animals**

   Who was in trouble?
   How did they escape?
   Who helped them escape?

2. **The Emperor and the Kite**

   Who was in trouble?
   How did he escape?
   Who helped him escape?

Now you be the author. The character in this picture is in trouble. Draw or tell a story about her "great escape" plan. Write a title for your story. Begin by telling *who* the character is and *how* her trouble began. Then tell *how* she escaped.

The Grasshopper

A poem by David McCord

Down

a

deep

well

a

grasshopper

fell.

By kicking about
He thought to get out.

He might have known better,
For that got him wetter.

Pictures by Julie Peterson

To kick round and round
Is the way to get drowned,
     And drowning is what
     I should tell you he got.
          But
          the
          well
          had
          a
          rope
          that
          dangled
          some
          hope.

And sure as molasses

On one of his passes

   He found the rope handy

   And up he went, *and he*

      it

      up

      and

      it

      up

      and

      it

      up

      and

      it

      up

      went

And hopped away proper

As any grasshopper.

Not Me

A poem by Shel Silverstein

The Slithergadee has crawled out of the sea.
He may catch all the others, but he
   won't catch me.
No, you won't catch me, Old Slithergadee,
You may catch all the others, but you wo—

Picture by Robert Evans

217

My Father
and the Dragon

From the story *My Father's Dragon* by Ruth Stiles Gannett
Pictures by Don Weller

218

My father had an exciting adventure when he was a boy—all because he found an alley cat who told him about a baby dragon. The cat had been on Wild Island when the dragon fell from a low cloud and injured a wing. The animals of Wild Island captured the small dragon easily. Then the lazy animals began forcing the dragon to fly them across the river that divided their island since the crocodiles in the river could not be trusted.

My father set out to rescue the dragon. First he sneaked aboard a ship bound for the Island of Tangerina. From there he went to Wild Island, where he had to outwit many animals who wanted to eat him. At last he got to the river. He knew the baby dragon was on the other side.

My father walked back and forth along the bank trying to think of some way to cross the river. He found a high flagpole with a rope going over to the other side. The rope went through a loop at the top of the pole and then down the pole and around a large crank. A sign on the crank said:

To Summon Dragon,
Yank the Crank
Report Disorderly Conduct
To Gorilla.

From what the cat had told my father, he knew that the other end of the rope was tied around the dragon's neck. And he felt sorrier than ever for the poor dragon. If the dragon was on this side, the gorilla would twist his wings. It would hurt so much that he'd have to fly to the other side. If he was on the other side, the gorilla would crank the rope until the dragon would either choke to death or fly back to this side. What a life for a baby dragon!

agon,
ank

My father knew that if he called to the
dragon to come across the river, the gorilla
would surely hear him. So he thought about
climbing the pole and going across on the
rope. The pole was very high. Even if he
could get to the top without being seen, he'd
have to go all the way across hand over
hand. The river was very muddy. All sorts of
unfriendly things might live in it. But my father
could think of no other way to get across.
He was about to start up the pole when,
despite all the noise the monkeys were
making, he heard a loud splash behind him.
He looked all around in the water. But it was
dusk now, and he couldn't see anything there.

"It's me. Crocodile," said a voice to the left. "The water's lovely. And I have such a craving for something sweet. Won't you come in for a swim?"

A pale moon came out from behind the clouds. My father could now see where the voice was coming from. The crocodile's head was just peeping out of the water.

"Oh, no thank you," said my father. "I never swim after sundown. But I do have something sweet to offer you. Perhaps you'd like a lollipop. And perhaps you have friends who would like lollipops, too?"

"Lollipops!" said the crocodile. "Why, that is a treat! How about it, boys?"

A whole chorus of voices shouted, "Hurrah! Lollipops!" My father counted as many as seventeen crocodiles with their heads just peeping out of the water.

"That's fine," said my father. And he got out the two dozen pink lollipops and the rubber bands. "I'll stick one here in the bank. Lollipops last longer if you keep them out of the water, you know. Now, one of you can have this one."

The crocodile who had first spoken swam up and tasted it. "Delicious, mighty delicious!" he said.

"Now if you don't mind," said my father, "I'll just walk along your back and fasten another lollipop to the tip of your tail with a rubber band. You don't mind, do you?"

"Oh, no, not in the least," said the crocodile.

"Can you get your tail out of the water just a bit?" asked my father.

"Yes, of course," said the crocodile, and he lifted up his tail. Then my father ran along his back and fastened another lollipop with a rubber band.

"Who's next?" said my father. A second crocodile swam up and began sucking on that lollipop.

"Now, you gentlemen can save a lot of time if you just line up across the river," said my father. "I'll be along to give you each a lollipop."

So the crocodiles lined up right across the river. With their tails in the air, they waited for my father to fasten on the rest of the lollipops. The tail of the seventeenth crocodile just reached the other bank.

My father was crossing the back of the fifteenth crocodile with two more lollipops to go, when the noise of the monkeys suddenly stopped. He could hear a much bigger noise getting louder every second. Then he could hear seven furious tigers and one raging rhinoceros and two seething lions and one ranting gorilla along with countless screeching monkeys. They were led by two extremely angry wild boars. All were yelling, "It's a trick! It's a trick! There's an invasion and it must be after our dragon. Kill it! Kill it!" The whole crowd stampeded down to the bank.

As my father was fixing the seventeenth lollipop for the last crocodile, he heard a wild boar scream, "Look, it came this way! It's over there now, see! The crocodiles made a bridge for it." And just as my father leapt onto the other bank, one of the wild boars jumped onto the back of the first crocodile. My father didn't have a moment to spare.

By now the dragon realized that my father was coming to rescue him. He ran out of the bushes and jumped up and down yelling, "Here I am! I'm right here! Can you see me? Hurry, the boar is coming over on the crocodiles, too. They're all coming over! Oh, please hurry, hurry!" The noise was simply terrible.

My father ran up to the dragon and took out his very sharp jackknife. "Steady, old boy, steady. We'll make it. Just stand still," he told the dragon as he began to saw through the big rope.

By this time both boars, all seven tigers, the two lions, the rhinoceros, and the gorilla, along with the countless screeching monkeys, were all on their way across the crocodiles. And there was still a lot of rope to cut through.

"Oh, hurry," the dragon kept saying. My father again told him to stand still.

"If I don't think I can make it," said my father, "we'll fly over to the other side of the river. I can finish cutting the rope there."

Suddenly the screaming grew louder and madder. My father thought the animals must have crossed the river. He looked around, and saw something which surprised and delighted him. Partly because he had finished his lollipop, and partly because, as I told you before, crocodiles are very moody and not the least bit dependable and are always looking for something to eat, the first crocodile had turned away from the bank. He had started swimming down the river. The second crocodile hadn't finished yet. So he followed right after the first, still sucking his lollipop. All the rest did the same thing, one right after the other, until they were all swimming away in a line. The two wild boars, the seven tigers, the rhinoceros, the two lions, the gorilla, along with the countless screeching monkeys, were all riding down the middle of the river on the train of crocodiles sucking pink lollipops, and all were yelling and screaming and getting their feet wet.

My father and the dragon laughed themselves weak because it was such a silly sight. As soon as they had recovered, my father finished cutting the rope. The dragon raced around in circles and tried to turn a somersault. He was the most excited baby dragon that ever lived. My father was in a hurry to fly away. When the dragon finally calmed down a bit, my father climbed up onto his back.

"All aboard!" said the dragon. "Where shall we go?"

"We'll spend the night on the beach. Tomorrow we'll start on the long journey home. So, it's off to the shores of Tangerina!" shouted my father. The dragon soared above the dark jungle and the muddy river and all the animals bellowing at them and all the crocodiles licking pink lollipops and grinning wide grins.

Questions

1. How do you summon a dragon in this story?

2. What do you give a crocodile that likes sweets?

3. How do you cross a river in this story?

4. What would you do with a dragon if you got to Tangerina?

Activity

Help Glinda finish her story. Add describing words and nonsense words. Make the story funny!

"You can't catch me!" I yelled.
Then I started to run. Behind
me were—
    Four _____ plum-zoomers,
    Three laughing _____,
    Two _____ duffle-wompers,
    And one _____ _____.
    And they all caught me.

BOOKSHELF

Wiley and the Hairy Man by Molly Garrett Bang. Macmillan, 1976. When Wiley goes out on the Tombigbee River, he meets the Hairy Man. Wiley must find a way to escape from this hairy beast.

The Angry Moon by William Sleator. Little, Brown, 1970. Lupan climbs into the sky on an arrow ladder to try to rescue his friend from the angry moon.

Little Tim and the Brave Sea Captain by Edward Ardizzone. Henry Z. Walck, 1955. Tim stows away aboard a ship and proves his courage during a storm at sea.

Petronella by Jay Williams. Parents' Magazine Press, 1973. Like her two brothers, Petronella sets out on an adventure. She, however, is looking for a prince to rescue.

The Three Wishes: A Collection of Puerto Rican Folktales retold by Ricardo E. Alegría. Harcourt, Brace & World, 1969. Princesses and clever animals escape from danger in these fine tales.

5 Would You Believe It!

Talk

A West African folk tale retold by Harold Courlander and George Herzog
Pictures by Sarn Suvityasiri

Once, not far from the city of Accra on the
Gulf of Guinea, a country man went out to his
garden to dig up some yams to take to market.
While he was digging, one of the yams said to
him:

"Well, at last you're here. You never
weeded me, but now you come around with
your digging stick. Go away and leave me
alone!"

The farmer turned around and looked at his
cow in amazement. The cow was chewing her
cud and looking at him.

"Did you say something?" he asked.

The cow kept on chewing and said nothing, but the man's dog spoke up.

"It wasn't the cow who spoke to you," the dog said. "It was the yam. The yam says to leave him alone."

The man became angry, because his dog had never talked before, and he didn't like his tone besides. So he took his knife and cut a branch from a palm tree to whip his dog. Just then the palm tree said:

"Put that branch down!"

The man was getting very upset about the way things were going, and he started to throw the palm branch away, but the palm branch said:

"Man, put me down softly!"

He put the branch down gently on a stone, and the stone said:

"Hey, take that thing off me!"

This was enough, and the frightened farmer started to run for his village. On the way he met a fisherman going the other way with a fish trap on his head.

"What's the hurry?" the fisherman asked.

"My yam said, 'Leave me alone!' Then the dog said, 'Listen to what the yam says!' When I went to whip the dog with a palm branch the tree said, 'Put that branch down!' Then the palm branch said, 'Do it softly!' Then the stone said, 'Take that thing off me!'"

"Is that all?" the man with the fish trap asked. "Is that so frightening?"

"Well," the man's fish trap said, "did he take it off the stone?"

"Wah!" the fisherman shouted. He threw the fish trap on the ground and began to run with the farmer, and on the trail they met a weaver with a bundle of cloth on his head.

"Where are you going in such a rush?" he asked them.

"My yam said, 'Leave me alone!'" the farmer said. "The dog said, 'Listen to what the yam says!' The tree said, 'Put that branch down!' The branch said, 'Do it softly!' And the stone said, 'Take that thing off me!'"

"And then," the fisherman continued, "the fish trap said, 'Did he take it off?'"

"That's nothing to get excited about," the weaver said, "no reason at all."

"Oh yes it is," his bundle of cloth said. "If it happened to you you'd run too!"

"Wah!" the weaver shouted. He threw his bundle on the trail and started running with the other men.

They came panting to the ford in the river
and found a man bathing.

"Are you chasing a gazelle?" he asked them.

The first man said breathlessly:

"My yam talked at me, and it said, 'Leave
me alone!' And my dog said, 'Listen to your
yam!' And when I cut myself a branch the tree
said, 'Put that branch down!' And the branch
said, 'Do it softly!' And the stone said, 'Take
that thing off me!'"

The fisherman panted:

"And my trap said, 'Did he?'"

The weaver wheezed:

"And my bundle of cloth said, 'You'd run too!'"

"Is that why you're running?" the man in the river asked.

"Well, wouldn't you run if you were in their position?" the river said.

The man jumped out of the water and began to run with the others. They ran down the main street of the village to the house of the chief. The chief's servants brought his stool out, and he came and sat on it to listen to their complaints. The men began to recite their troubles.

"I went out to my garden to dig yams," the farmer said, waving his arms. "Then everything began to talk! My yam said, 'Leave me alone!' My dog said, 'Pay attention to your yam!' The tree said, 'Put that branch down!' The branch said, 'Do it softly!' And the stone said, 'Take it off me!'"

"And my fish trap said, 'Well, did he take it off?'" the fisherman said.

"And my cloth said, 'You'd run too!'" the weaver said.

"And the river said the same," the bather said hoarsely, his eyes bulging.

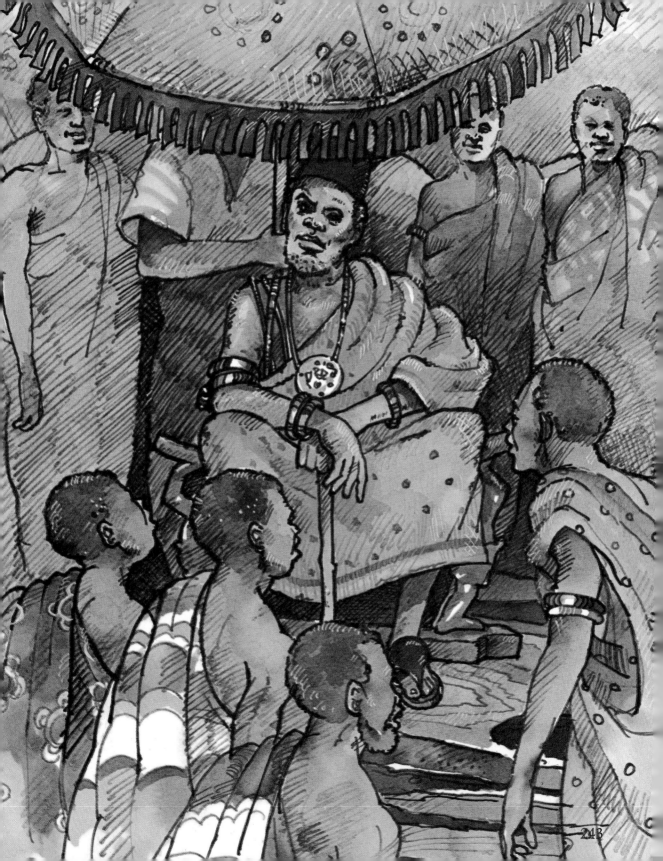

The chief listened to them patiently, but he couldn't refrain from scowling.

"Now this is really a wild story," he said at last. "You'd better all go back to your work before I punish you for disturbing the peace."

So the men went away, and the chief shook his head and mumbled to himself, "Nonsense like that upsets the community."

"Fantastic, isn't it?" his stool said. "Imagine, a talking yam!"

Questions

1. You know this story is funny because
    a. yams need weeding.   b. yams don't talk.
          c. yams taste good.

2. Tell what might have happened after the chief's stool spoke.

3. Find the words used in the story instead of the underlined words.
    a. The chief listened to the men's <u>talk</u>.
    b. The men began to <u>tell</u> their troubles.

Activity

Suppose you are getting ready to tell the story "Talk." Here is a plan to help you remember the first part of the story.

The yam talks. → The dog talks. → The tree talks. → ?

Complete this plan for the rest of the story. Remember to list the things in the order in which they happened.

Mrs. Beggs and the Wizard

Story and pictures by Mercer Mayer

One day a stranger appeared at Mrs. Beggs's boarding house looking for a room to rent. His calling card read

Z. P. ALABASIUM

Wizard Extraordinaire.

"This room suits me fine," he said. "I'll take it." He gave Mrs. Beggs a month's deposit and she gave him the key.

That evening Mr. Alabasium didn't show up for dinner, so Mrs. Beggs fixed him a tray of food and took it up to his room.

"Just leave it on the floor, Mrs. Beggs," he said, not bothering to open the door.

"Dear me," she said and went down the stairs.

That night as she lay in bed, she heard strange noises from the room above. Up the stairs crept Mrs. Beggs, followed closely by all the guests who had also heard the noises.

"Oh my, what can be happening?" she said, knocking on Mr. Alabasium's door.

"Nothing to concern yourself with, Mrs. Beggs," said Mr. Alabasium. "Now leave me be." With that he slammed the door shut.

That would have suited Mrs. Beggs just
fine, for she wasn't a particularly nosy
person. However, the next morning she
found the fresh cut flowers on the dining
room table withered and dead. Oh well, I'll
cut some more, she thought, and went outside.

In the backyard, her beautiful garden
was overgrown with weeds, thistles, and
briars. To make matters worse, the birdbath
was full of toads. As if that wasn't enough, a
giant windstorm came up that afternoon just
as Mrs. Beggs was hanging out the laundry.
With a swoosh and a swirl, Mrs. Beggs and
the fresh clean laundry were blown all over
the yard.

But even stranger things were yet to happen.

The following day a rainstorm thundered
through the parlor, soaking everyone to the
bone.

"Oh, I'm sorry," cried Mrs. Beggs. "It has
never rained in here before."

At lunch the tables and chairs floated
through the air. The dishes and fine china
fell off the shelves.

Strange things wandered through the house or just floated through the air frightening the guests. Mr. Plimp's beaver hat turned back into a beaver and bit Mr. Plimp on the nose. Mrs. Fizzle found reptiles in her bed.

Needless to say, the guests were very unhappy and complained.

To make matters even worse, a blizzard
raged into the house, howling and blowing
snow everywhere.

"Mrs. Beggs," said Major Clearlob, "I
believe I can speak for the rest of the
guests. That Mr. Alabasium is up to no good.
Either he goes or we go."

Oh dear, thought Mrs. Beggs. This is becoming very bad for business. I must find out if Mr. Alabasium is up to no good or not.

"Mr. Alabasium," she said knocking on his door, "I was wondering if . . . " But before she finished talking she found herself dressed in a ballet costume, standing on a giant turtle.

"Oh dear," she said. "This must stop."
So she called the constable.

The constable came and knocked on the
door.

"Open up, this is the constable."

Suddenly the constable turned into a ram.

"Baaaaaaaaa," he said and ran down the
stairs.

"That does it," Mrs. Beggs said angrily. She went to her closet. She opened the door. Reaching high up in the closet she pulled down an old tattered box from the top shelf.

This may not be the right thing to do, she thought, but one must do something. The top of the box read

WITCHERY FOR FUN AND PROFIT.

It had belonged to her great aunt Celia, who flew away on a vacuum cleaner one day—not having any broomsticks on hand—and was never seen again.

Mrs. Beggs put on the costume, which was a little too large, and sat down to read the instruction booklet.

"There," she said. "I hope this will do the trick." Then she chanted, ever so quietly,

> *"I've had blizzards,*
>
> *Snakes and lizards.*
>
> *I've had rain and wind to bear."*

As she spoke, the room filled with smoke.

> *"I've heard noises and lots of howling,*
>
> *Tables floating through the air."*

Bats darted through the room and strange things peered from the dark.

> *"Powers creeping, I command you,*
>
> *Get that wizard out of here!"*

With a howl the roomful of strange things dashed through the window and were gone. Putting everything neatly away, Mrs. Beggs went to bed.

Later that evening Mr. Alabasium slept well.
The window to his room slid slowly open.
Quietly, ever so quietly, in crept a group
of very strange things. They tied him up with
a wizard-proof rope. They tickled his toes

and tweaked his nose. They carried him
quietly out of the house and through the
back streets of the town. They left Z. P.
ALABASIUM, *Wizard Extraordinaire,* at the
city dump and flew off in the night.

The next day, when nothing strange happened at the boarding house, the guests were overjoyed.

"My, my, it's so very peaceful around here," commented Mrs. Fizzle.

"It most certainly is," replied the other guests, smiling their approval.

By late afternoon, Major Clearlob sighed and said, "It's far too peaceful around here. I'm bored to tears."

"So are we," the others replied.

At dinnertime all the guests quietly sipped their soup. Then the doorbell rang.

"I wonder who that could be at this hour," said Mrs. Beggs, and she went to answer the door.

Questions

Be Mr. Z. P. Alabasium. Answer the first three questions for him.

1. Give two reasons why Mrs. Beggs wanted to get rid of you.

2. Why did you do those strange things at Mrs. Beggs's house? (Make up this answer.)

3. Where were you at the end of the story? (Make up this answer.)

4. *Swoosh* and *swirl* are two words that tell about sounds and actions in the story. Find four more such words in the story.

Activity

At the end of the story, Major Clearlob said, "I'm bored to tears," but the last picture shows that he was in for a surprise. What, do you think, was the surprise? Write what you think happened.

Adventures of Isabel

From the poem by Ogden Nash

Isabel met an enormous bear,

Isabel, Isabel, didn't care.

The bear was hungry, the bear was ravenous,

The bear's big mouth was cruel and cavernous.

The bear said, Isabel, glad to meet you,

How do, Isabel, now I'll eat you!

Isabel, Isabel, didn't worry;

Isabel didn't scream or scurry.

She washed her hands and she straightened her
   hair up,

Then Isabel quietly ate the bear up.

Picture by Susan Jaekel

The Big Wind of '34

A tall tale by James Flora
Pictures by Marie-Louise Gay

If you stay around Grandpa long enough, you will hear all sorts of amazing stories about his farm. Some people might call them tall tales, but you can decide for yourself after reading this tale as Grandpa tells it.

When Grandma and I first came to the farm, there was no barn—just a house. We were very poor and couldn't afford to build a barn. We had a cow, and she had to sleep outside. She didn't like that at all. On cold days she would get so angry that she wouldn't give us any milk.

We tried to explain to the cow how sorry we were, but she wouldn't listen. When a cow gets good and mad, she just won't listen to anybody.

Then one day in 1934 the wind started to blow. Oh, my! How it did blow! Harder and harder until it blew all the leaves off the trees. Stronger and stronger until it blew the trees away, too. I had to tie down the cow or she would have been carried away. Even so, she sailed around in the sky like a big cow kite.

I've never seen such a strong wind in my whole life. I had just finished digging a deep well in the backyard. I had to dig it down forty feet, and that was hard work. But that wind huffed and puffed until it blew the well right out of the ground and carried it away. I never did see it again.

That made me so mad that I ran out of
the house and threw a big chunk of
firewood at the wind. It must have hurt
him. It must have made him stop and think
how mean he was being to Grandma and
me, because the next thing I saw was a big
blue barn sailing through the air. It
swished over the house and settled there
where you see it now. It was a good barn,
but it didn't have any doors. So I shouted:

"HEY, WIND! YOU FORGOT THE
DOORS!"

That old wind turned right around and blew back to wherever he had come from. In no time at all, I could hear him coming back. Sure enough, he had the doors for the barn. And he even fetched the pigeon house you see on top.

When the wind had gone, I went out and looked around that fine barn. It was just what I wanted. The only trouble was that it had settled on our cow's tail and broken it off. That made me very sad, but Grandma said not to worry. She said she had cow salve that would fix everything. But that's another story, which I will tell you some day.

Questions

1. List two things the Big Wind of '34 did.

2. Grandma says, "Grandpa told a *tall tale* about the wind." What does she mean?
   a. His story was wild and not to be believed.
   b. His story really did happen.
   c. His story was about a long-tailed animal.

3. Which cow would you find in a *tall tale?*
   a. A cow that hid behind a bush.
   b. A cow that gave orange juice, not milk.
   c. A cow that frightened away a robber.

4. Grandma said she would put *salve* on the cow's tail. Is salve a string, a kind of medicine, or an extra tail?

Activity

Grandpa told a tall tale about 1934. Write an exciting *tall tale title* for this year: "The _____ of _____." Draw or paint a picture to go with your title.

Eat-It-All Elaine

A poem by Kaye Starbird

I went away last August
To summer camp in Maine,
And there I met a camper
Called Eat-it-all Elaine.
Although Elaine was quiet,
She liked to cause a stir
By acting out the nickname
Her camp-mates gave to her.

The day of our arrival
At Cabin Number Three
When girls kept coming over
To greet Elaine and me,
She took a piece of paper
And calmly chewed it up,
Then strolled outside the cabin
And ate a buttercup.

Elaine, from that day forward,
Was always in command.
On hikes, she'd eat some birch-bark.
On swims, she'd eat some sand.
At meals, she'd swallow prune-pits
And never have a pain,
While everyone around her
Would giggle, "Oh Elaine!"

One morning, berry-picking,
A bug was in her pail,
And though we thought for certain
Her appetite would fail,
Elaine said, "Hmm, a stinkbug."
And while we murmured, "Ooh,"
She ate her pail of berries
And ate the stinkbug, too.

Pictures by Marie-Louise Gay

271

The night of Final Banquet
When counselors were handing
Awards to different children
Whom they believed outstanding,
To every *thinking* person
At summer camp in Maine
The Most Outstanding Camper
Was Eat-it-all Elaine.

BOOKSHELF

Tell Me a Mitzi by Lore Segal. Farrar, Straus & Giroux, 1970. Mitzi tells three funny stories about her family.

The Tsar's Riddles or the Wise Little Girl retold by Guy Daniels. McGraw-Hill, 1967. An argument between a rich man and his poor brother is to be settled by answering the Tsar's riddles.

The Adventures of Spider retold by Joyce Cooper Arkhurst. Little, Brown, 1964. "How Spider Got a Thin Waist" and the other stories in this book tell about the adventures of clever Spider.

Mr. Yowder and the Steamboat by Glen Rounds. Holiday House, 1977. When Mr. Yowder visits New York City and decides to go fishing, he causes one problem after the other.

The Stars in the Sky by Joseph Jacobs. Farrar, Straus & Giroux, 1979. A young girl wants the stars in the sky as toys. She dreams about her wish being granted.

6 There Is
a Season...

The Twelve Months

A Russian folk tale retold by Moura Budberg and
Amabel Williams-Ellis
Pictures by Kinuko Craft

Do you know how many months there are in
a year?

Twelve.

What are they?

January, February, March, April, May, June,
July, August, September, October, November,
December.

As soon as one month ends, the next one
begins. February has never once, not once, come
before January, or May before April.

One follows the other, and they never meet.

But people say that in the hilly country of
Bohemia there was a little girl who once saw all
the twelve months at the same time.

How did that come about?

It came about this way.

In a small village there lived a wicked woman who had a daughter and a stepdaughter. She loved her daughter, but the stepdaughter could do nothing to please her. Whatever she did was wrong. Whichever way she turned it was in the wrong direction.

The daughter lay in bed the whole day long eating gingerbread. But the stepdaughter worked from morning till night—fetching water or carrying wood from the forest, or washing linen in the river, or weeding in the orchard.

She felt the bitter cold of the winter, the broiling heat of the summer, the fresh winds of spring, and the autumn rains. Perhaps that is why she managed to see all the twelve months at the same time.

It was winter, the middle of January. There was so much snow that it had to be cleared away from the doors. And in the forest, trees stood up to their waists in snowdrifts and couldn't even sway when the wind pushed them.

People kept indoors and sat by their stoves.

On such a day, towards nightfall, the wicked stepmother opened the door and saw the snowstorm raging. Then she returned to the warm fire and said to her stepdaughter, "You ought to go to the forest and pick some snowdrops. Tomorrow is your sister's birthday."

The little girl glanced at her stepmother. Was she joking, or was she really sending her into the forest? It would be terrifying to go to the forest in weather like this. And what snowdrops could there be in the middle of winter? They never appeared before March, no matter where you looked for them. It would be easy to get lost in the forest, or to sink in the snowdrifts.

Her stepsister said to her, "Even if you do get lost, who is there to worry about you? Go, and don't come back without the flowers. Here, take the basket."

The girl burst into tears. But she wrapped herself in a torn shawl and left the house. The wind tore at the shawl and threw snowflakes into her eyes as she walked through the snowdrifts.

It grew darker and darker. The sky was black, and there was not a single star to peer down at the white earth below.

She came to the forest. Now it was quite dark, and she couldn't even see her hands. The girl sat on the stump of a tree. If she must freeze to death, what difference would it make where she waited?

Suddenly a light flashed far away among the trees—as if a star had got caught among the branches.

The girl stood up again and began to struggle towards the light. Often she sank in the snow. Often she had to climb over fallen trees. I mustn't lose the light, she kept thinking to herself. The light became brighter and still brighter. Now she could catch the scent of warm smoke. She could hear the crackling of logs burning in a fire.

On she hurried and soon she came to a clearing in the forest. And here she stood stock still, for it was suddenly very bright as if the sun were shining. There was a huge bonfire burning in the middle of the clearing, with flames reaching almost to the sky. And there were people, some near the bonfire, some farther away. They were talking quietly among themselves.

The girl looked at them and wondered who they could be. They didn't look like hunters and certainly not like woodcutters—they were so beautifully dressed, some in silver, some in gold, some in green velvet.

She began to count and she counted twelve: three old people, three middle-aged, three young ones, and the last three were just boys.

The young ones sat close by the fire, the older ones farther away.

Suddenly one old man turned round—the tallest one, with a long beard and bushy eyebrows—and saw the girl. She was frightened and wanted to run but it was too late. The old man asked her loudly, "Where did you come from? What do you want?"

The little girl showed her empty basket and said, "I've got to pick some snowdrops and put them in my basket."

The old man laughed. "Snowdrops in January! What an idea!"

"It's not my idea," the girl replied. "My stepmother sent me here for them and told me not to come back with an empty basket."

The twelve men glanced at her then and began to whisper among themselves. The girl stood there listening, but she could not make out what they were saying. It was as though it were not people speaking at all, but the trees rustling.

They whispered and whispered and then they stopped.

The tall old man turned to her again and asked, "What will you do if you don't find the snowdrops? They won't appear before March, you know."

"I must stay in the forest," answered the girl. "I'll wait for March. It would be better to freeze to death in the woods than to go home without the snowdrops."

She said this and burst into tears.

Suddenly the youngest of the twelve rose to his feet and walked up to the old man.

"Brother January," he said, "let me come in your place for an hour."

The old man stroked his long beard and said, "I would do it willingly, but March can't come before February."

"It's all right," murmured another old man, very shaggy, with an untidy beard. "You can let him come in your place for an hour. I won't argue! We all of us know this child. We've seen her sometimes at the river with her pails, or in the forest gathering a handful of wood. She's one of us. She belongs to all of us, to all the months, so we must help her now."

"So be it," said old January.

He struck his ice-ax and said:

> "Frosts keep away
> From the trees in the forest,
> Leave the core
> Of the birch, or the pine.
> Freeze neither the ravens
> Nor houses of men!"

He fell silent and silence came to the forest too. The trees stopped crackling and the snow fell in large, soft flakes.

"Now it's your turn, friend," said January, and handed the ax to his younger brother, shaggy February.

He struck his ax again, shook his beard and howled:

"Winds, gales, storms,
Blow as hard as you can,
Rage the whole night long.
Whistle in the chimneys,
Drum in the skies,
Twist and turn over the earth
Like a great white snake."

And as soon as he had said this a wet, stormy wind began to blow and shook the branches. The snowflakes whirled and whirled and raced over the earth. February handed his ax to his younger brother and said, "Your turn, brother March."

March hit the ground with his ax.

The girl stared and saw that it wasn't an ax any longer; it was a large branch, covered with buds.

March threw back his head and laughed, and began to sing loudly in his clear, young voice:

> "Streams, flow merrily,
> Pools, overflow,
> Come out, little ants
> And warm yourselves
> After winter's chill.
> The bear is leaving his lair
> And strolls in the forest;
> The birds are singing
> And the snowdrops are pushing
> through the earth."

The little girl clapped her hands in surprise. Where had the snowdrifts gone to? Where were the icicles hanging from every branch?

There was soft, fresh earth beneath her feet. All round her she heard the ripple of running water, and the sound of melting snow. The buds on the branches were bursting and green leaves pushed out of their dark skins.

The girl could hardly believe her eyes.

"You mustn't stand and stare," said March to her. "You must hurry, for we have only an hour to do what we want!"

So the little girl stopped staring and rushed into the forest to search for snowdrops—and there were thousands of them! Under the bushes, under the stones, here, there, and everywhere she looked. She picked a whole basketful, filled her apron too, and hurried back to the clearing where the twelve brothers had sat round the fire.

But there was no more fire, and the brothers were gone. It was very light in the clearing, but now it was a different light—not from the fire, but from the full moon that had appeared above the forest trees.

She was sorry she had no one to thank, but as there was nothing else to do she ran off home. The moon lighted her way. She scarcely felt her feet under her until she reached the door. But she hardly had time to walk in before the snowstorm raged again and the moon vanished behind the clouds.

"Ah, so you're back already!" said her stepmother and sister. "Where are the snowdrops?"

The girl didn't reply but poured the snowdrops from her apron onto the bench and put the basket beside them.

The stepmother and sister were amazed.

"Where did you get them?"

The girl told them all that had happened. They listened and shook their heads, not knowing whether to believe her or not. It was hard to believe, but there were the snowdrops, all fresh and white, lying on the bench to remind one of March.

They exchanged sidelong glances, and the stepmother asked:

"Did the months give you anything else?"

"I didn't ask them for anything else."

"What a fool, what a fool!" said her stepsister. "To think that you met all twelve months at once and did not ask them for anything but snowdrops. Had I been in your place, I would have known what to ask for. I'd have asked one for apples and sweet pears, the other for ripe strawberries, the third for tasty mushrooms, the fourth for fresh cucumbers."

"There's a clever girl!" said the stepmother. "In the winter, strawberries and pears are beyond price. We might have sold them and for so much money! And this little fool brings nothing but snowdrops! Put on some warm clothes, my daughter, and go to the clearing. They won't pull the wool over *your* eyes, though there are twelve of them to your one."

"They certainly won't!" answered her daughter, her arms already in her sleeves and a kerchief over her head.

Her mother shouted after her, "Put on mittens, and button up your coat."

But the door had already closed behind her. She ran to the forest, following her sister's footsteps.

The sooner I get to the clearing, the better, she thought.

The forest was dense and dark, the snowdrifts high, rising like a wall.

Oh! thought the girl. Why on earth did I choose to come to the forest, instead of staying in my warm bed? I'm frozen to the bone and am sure to catch my death of cold!

Hardly were the words out of her mouth before she caught sight of a light in the distance—as if a star had got caught in the branches.

She went towards the light, struggling
through the snow, and finally came to the
clearing. A large woodpile was burning there and
around it sat the twelve months, softly talking to
one another.

She walked up to the fire. She did not bow
in greeting or say a kind word, but chose the best
spot and sat down to get warm.

The brothers fell silent. The forest was still.
Suddenly January struck his ax on the ground.

"Who are you?" he asked. "Where do you
come from?"

"From my house," the girl replied. "You have given my sister a large basket of snowdrops. So I came, following her footsteps."

"We know your sister," said January, "but we've never set eyes on you. What is the purpose of your visit?"

"I've come for presents. I want June to fill my basket with strawberries, and I'd like large ones too. And July could give me fresh cucumbers and white mushrooms, and August some sweet pears and apples. September could give me some ripe nuts. And October . . . "

"Wait a moment," said January. "Summer doesn't come before spring or spring before winter. It's a long way to go yet until the month of June. I'm January, the master of the forest now, and I shall reign here for thirty-one days."

"How disagreeable you are!" said the girl. "It's not you I came to see at all! There's nothing to get from you but snow and frost. It's the summer months I want."

January frowned. "Search for summer in the winter," he said.

He waved his great sleeve and a snowstorm blew up from the earth to the sky covering the trees and the clearing where the twelve brothers were sitting. One could not even see the fire for the snow. One could only hear it hissing somewhere, crackling and moaning.

The girl was suddenly terrified. "Stop!" she cried. "Stop! That's enough!"

But it was all in vain.

The snowstorm was whirling around her, blinding her, and she couldn't breathe. She fell down in a snowdrift and was buried under soft white snow.

The mother waited and waited for her daughter. She peered out of the window and rushed to the door, but there was no sign of her. So she wrapped herself up warmly and went to the forest. But how could she hope to find her child in such a storm! She walked and walked, and searched high and low, but she found nothing.

And so they stayed there, both of them in the forest, to wait for the coming of the summer.

The other girl lived on happily. She grew into a young woman, married, and had children.

And she had a garden round her house. People said that such a wondrous garden had never been seen before. Flowers bloomed there before anywhere else. Berries ripened. Pears and apples mellowed. It was cool in the heat of summer, quiet in a storm.

"All the months of the year seem to visit that young woman at once," people used to say.

And who knows? Perhaps it was the truth.

Questions

1. If you made this story into a play, what two places would you show on your stage?

2. Why did the Twelve Months treat the two girls differently?

3. In the story the stepmother said to her daughter, "They won't pull the wool over *your* eyes." What did she mean?
   a. They won't cover your face.
   b. They won't fool you.
   c. They won't let you get cold.

Activity

Like most folk tales, *The Twelve Months* is a story people made up long ago. Year after year, people told this story and passed it on to others. Give two reasons why people tell this tale again and again.

Winter Night

A poem by Harry Behn

It is very dark
But not late.
Not after eight.

The only light
Comes from snow
Beginning to show.

Bushes are first
As flakes fall,
Then the top of a wall.

What used to be dark
Is now a hill.
It is very still.

Picture by Christa Kieffer

A very fat snowman named Wheezer
Was truly a clever old geezer.
    Whenever he felt
    He was starting to melt,
He'd spend a few days in the freezer.

A limerick by Edward Mullins

Picture by Ed Taber

Winter Walk

A poem by Robert Froman

Cold sky, cold air, cold sidewalk, cold street.

Cold.

SHIVERS.

GOOSE pimples.

RUUUBBB HAAANDDDS.

STAMP FEET.

STILL COLD.

GO IN THIS STORE A MINUTE.

AHHHHHHHHH!

In Time of Silver Rain

A poem by Langston Hughes

In time of silver rain
The earth
Puts forth new life again,
Green grasses grow
And flowers lift their heads,
And over all the plain
The wonder spreads
Of life, of life, of life!

March

A poem by Elizabeth Coatsworth

A blue day,
a blue jay
and a good beginning.

One crow
melting snow—
spring's winning!

Spring

A poem by Karla Kuskin

I'm shouting
I'm singing
I'm swinging through trees
I'm winging skyhigh
With the buzzing black bees.
I'm the sun
I'm the moon
I'm the dew on the rose.
I'm a rabbit
Whose habit
Is twitching his nose.
I'm lively
I'm lovely
I'm kicking my heels.
I'm crying "Come dance"
To the fresh water eels.
I'm racing through meadows
Without any coat
I'm a gamboling lamb
I'm a light leaping goat.
I'm a bud
I'm a bloom
I'm a dove on the wing.
I'm running on rooftops
And welcoming spring!

Picture by Christa Kieffer

The Fourth

A poem by Shel Silverstein

Oh

CRASH!

my

BASH!

it's

BANG!

the

ZANG!

Fourth

WHOOSH!

of

BAROOOM!

July

WHEW!

Gently, gently, the wind blows
dandelions' parachutes
into the afternoon sun.

A poem by Kazue Mizumura

Pictures by Christa Kieffer

Fall

A haiku by Sally Andresen

The geese flying south
In a row long and V-shaped
Pulling in winter.

Spendthrift

A poem by Norma Farber

Coins—coins—coins—
      a bushel to a breeze—
are pouring from the pockets
      of the elm in the square.

Gather up the money heaps
      as many as you please.
So rich an old tree
      doesn't count them or care.

Theme in Yellow

A poem by Carl Sandburg

I spot the hills
With yellow balls in autumn.
I light the prairie cornfields
Orange and tawny gold clusters
And I am called pumpkins.
On the last of October
When dusk is fallen
Children join hands
And circle round me
Singing ghost songs
And love to the harvest moon;
I am a jack-o'-lantern
With terrible teeth
And the children know
I am fooling.

Pictures by Christa Kieffer

From

Along Sandy Trails

A story by Ann Nolan Clark
Photographs by Alfred A. Cohn

My grandmother tells me,
"Small Papago Indian,
girl of the Desert People,
for two summer moons
I will walk with you
across the sand patches,
by the rock ridges
and the cacti,
through the dry washes
and along the sandy trails
that you may know the desert
and hold its beauty
in your heart forever."

I walk with my grandmother
   along a sandy trail.
The sand beneath my feet
   is damp and cool
   because, last night
   while I was sleeping,
   clouds rained down
   upon our thirsty land.

Rain washed the flowers
   of all the cacti,
   the pincushion
   and the cholla
   (CHOH·yah),
   the hedgehog
   and the prickly pear.

We sit by the trail to rest.
Beside me a lizard's track
    is penciled lightly
    on the sand.
I touch it with my fingers.
I see a gila (HEE·lah) woodpecker
    pecking the trunk
    of a giant cactus.
If I listen . . . listen . . . listen,
    I will hear him pecking.

Along the trail
    a roadrunner runs
    all stretched out
    as if he cannot get
    to where he is going
    fast enough, soon enough.
I look and see. I listen and hear.
There are so many things
    in this quiet land.

But I like best the quail.
I watch them walking,
    their black plumes bobbing
    from their red bonnets.
They walk across the trail
    near my grandmother and me,
    so busy talking together
    they do not see us.

Quail do not hop
    as some birds do.
They walk elegantly
    with quick, small steps.
Other birds walk alone,
    but quail go everywhere
    with their families
    and their friends.
They go in coveys.

Then my grandmother says,
 "Down the trail a little distance
 I will show you something
 to remember always."
We walk along and come
 to a spreading creosote.

Under its branches, on the ground,
 in a round place
 lined with desert grass,
 is a quail's nest.
In the nest are many eggs.
One is broken.
I count them
 but do not touch them
 or make a noise of any kind.

My grandmother whispers,
 "Watch. Be still.
 See the guard quail
 sitting on the cholla,
 not eating,
 not talking,
 just sitting.
 Listen. If he calls
 cra-er, cra-er, cra-er,
 he is warning his covey
 of danger."

I like best the quail.
But my grandmother likes
    the giant cactus,
    standing tall and stark
    against the sky.
Giant cactus gives us
    many important things.
The rain water stored
    in its pleated trunk
    stays our thirst
    when the winds
    of the dry moon
    sweep across our land.
Its white and yellow flower-crowns
    ripen slowly to scarlet fruit
    that we gather
    and store as food
    for the time
    of the hunger moon.

Our baskets are filled
   with the ripe fruit
   of the giant cactus
   that we have gathered,
   my grandmother and I,
   and that now we take
   to my mother's house.
The sand beneath our feet
   is deep and shifting.
The way seems long
   and our baskets are heavy.
We walk and rest.
We walk and rest.
After a time of just resting,
   happy and quiet,
   Grandmother says, "Come,
   little granddaughter.
   The sun travels westward
   to make the day's ending.
   Your father has worked
   his fields.
   Your mother has woven
   her baskets.
   Nighttime is waiting."

Questions

1. Why did the grandmother and the granddaughter walk in the desert?

2. Name three ways in which the quail are different from most other birds.

3. Why do you think this story has the title *Along Sandy Trails?*

4. The girl talks about the giant cactus and the *hunger moon.* What is the hunger moon?
   a. A moon that is hungry.
   b. A time when people might be hungry.
   c. A time when the moon looks empty.

Activity

Trails are everywhere. They may be sidewalk trails or road trails or park trails. Make a map of a trail near your home. Draw arrows to show the path to follow. Draw and label pictures of things to see along your trail.

I Go Forth to Move About the Earth

A poem by Alonzo Lopez

I go forth to move about the earth.
I go forth as the owl, wise and knowing.
I go forth as the eagle, powerful and bold.
I go forth as the dove, peaceful and gentle.
I go forth to move about the earth
    in wisdom, courage, and peace.

BOOKSHELF

Elephant Boy by William Kotzwinkle. Farrar, Straus & Giroux, 1970. A Stone Age boy learns how to live in his changing world.

A Child's Book of Seasons by Satomi Ichikawa. Parents' Magazine Press, 1975. Here is a book that pictures things to do ''in snow and sunshine, wind and rain, the changing seasons through.''

More Small Poems by Valerie Worth. Farrar, Straus & Giroux, 1976. Ordinary sights— sidewalks, toads, acorns—are seen in a new way in these poems.

City in the Winter by Eleanor Schick. Macmillan, 1970. A snowstorm closes school for the day. Jimmy and Grandmother spend the day doing all the things they never have time to do.

Turtle Pond by Berniece Freschet. Charles Scribner's Sons, 1971. When baby turtles hatch and hurry toward the pond, many dangers are waiting for them.

D 4
E 5
F 6
G 7
H 8
I 9
J 0